JUST TALK TO ME. . .

JUST TALK TO ME...

FROM PRIVATE VOICE TO PUBLIC SPEAKER

PETER SETTELEN

Thorsons
An Imprint of HarperCollinsPublishers

The author is grateful to the following for permission to quote from their works:

Uncle Vanya by Anton Chekov, translated by Elisaveta Fen,
Society of Authors, Penguin

Epitaph for George Dillon by John Osborne, David Higham Associates, Faber &
Faber

Look Back in Anger by John Osborne, David Higham Associates, Faber & Faber

Guilt and Gingerbread by Lionel Hale (attempts to locate the copyright holder
having failed, the author would be grateful of any information; please write
c/o the publisher)

Thorsons
An Imprint of HarperCollins*Publishers*
77–85 Fulham Palace Road
Hammersmith, London W6 8JB
1160 Battery Street
San Francisco, California 94111–1213

Published by Thorsons 1995
10 9 8 7 6 5 4 3 2 1

A catalogue record for this book
is available from the British Library

ISBN 0 7225 3005 6

Printed in Great Britain by
HarperCollinsManufacturing Glasgow

For Sarah
Who came into my life and loved me.
I couldn't have done it without you.

In memory of a little girl called Penny who gave me her life
and a little boy called Peter who showed me who I am.

When the child comes out to play
What do they do and what do they say?

ACKNOWLEDGEMENTS

I'd like to thank Ali, Alice, Andrew, Angela, Brian, Brian, Carolyn, Christine, Clare, Clive, Elaine, Esmond, Francesca, Francis, Jill, Jacquie, James, Jerome, Jill, John, Jonathan, Joseph, Lucy, Maria, Mary, Mitch, Rita, Roger, Sandy, Steve, Tara, Tom, Tom, Trish, Veronica and Vicky for being there with their love and affection all through the difficult times; Penny and John for believing in me at the beginning; Susie, Carolan and Steve for recommending me; Jane for believing I had something to say, Andrew for the time he gave to creating the cover and Lizzie for caringly editing my finished text; Richard for being my agent whatever I did and for telling me to write the book and Fiona for holding my hand while I did it. I'd like to thank Sylvia and Barry for giving me a place in the sun to work out what I was going to say; Maya for being my companion through the long days and nights in front of the processor and all my friends who forgave me for not coming out to play for months on end.
I'd also like to thank all those people who trusted me to unlock something they knew was there, but hadn't been able to reach on their own: their potential to be truly heard. Thank you for sharing your fears, thank you for sharing your passion. I learnt as much from each of you as I hope you learnt in return.

We teach what we need to learn.

CONTENTS

INTRODUCTION

There's an expression that rolls off the tongue so easily: 'Sticks and stones may break my bones, but words can never hurt me.' Nothing could be further from the truth. What you say to another human being and what they say to you has the most powerful effect on you both. We're truly able to move mountains with words. And the power of words can destroy people's lives. It really does matter what we say to each other and how we say it.

I recently went skiing with my wife Sarah. It was the first time for nearly 30 years. Of course I wasn't really fit enough and had been lazy about my preparation! An hour before we were due to finish our week on the piste, I fell and tore the ligaments in my knee. As I sit here, some weeks later, having had to cancel my clients, unable to move around with any ease, I've finally come to my desk to talk to you. For that's what I've realized it's going to be. A very private conversation with you, the person on the other side of these words.

When I act for television or film, people say to me, 'Don't you miss an audience?' I reply, 'But they're there. The moment I speak is the moment they see me and hear me. They're there.'

So the moment I write these words is the moment you read them. You're my next client, the next person to walk through my door. Someone whom I've never met before, someone who's had the courage to admit they find it hard to communicate as well as they'd like. Maybe you're a TV journalist, a newscaster or a presenter.

Maybe you work in the business world or are a public figure. Maybe you wish you could be more effective in meetings or you simply wish you were taken more seriously by the people around you. Maybe you suffer from drop-dead gut-wrenching fear at the thought of standing up in front of 3,000 people and giving a speech – or even having a truly intimate conversation with someone you love. Or maybe you just want to be heard. It really doesn't matter what you do or who you are, just that you have a need to express yourself more honestly and openly than you ever thought possible.

How can you learn to do this? All that seems to be offered is courses on how to prepare your 'material', how to hide your fear, how to fake what you feel. 'These are the skills of the actor,' so you're told, 'the professional liar. Stand with your feet apart and take three deep breaths. Don't wave your arms about and don't shuffle. Smile a lot. Be sincere, even if you don't believe what you're saying, and project.'

What are the results of this approach? These 'skills' are taken back into people's lives and used on us all. Scripts are learnt, phrases 'constructed' to have the greatest effect. A terrible sing-song of sound batters our emotions as the phrases and words lose all their meaning. 'Have a nice day' turns into a monster. A sea of insincerity fills our lives. And what does it succeed in doing? We feel more and more isolated, more and more disconnected. No one seems to be talking to anyone anymore. Words come out of people's mouths, but they don't mean a thing. We don't believe a single word they say!

Even the media has been infected, destroying the chance for many young newscasters and presenters to ever fulfil their true potential. They're left to copy the rhythms and tones of someone who's currently successful, with little understanding of why they're doing it. Today, there are those who will describe the deaths of thousands as if they were telling us 'it's going to be sunny in the south' – emphasizing every fourth word, whatever it is!

Also, we now have a generation of politicians who represent the worst excesses of insincerity, imagining we believe what they say when they slickly twist our truths for their own political gain.

How I long for them all to be honest, to talk to me – from the heart.

I've been described as a voice coach. What I actually do is to help people to communicate what they truly want to say, which isn't quite the same thing!

I trained as an actor at the London Academy of Music and Dramatic Art in London over 20 years ago. I started my acting career in television with occasional forays into the theatre, firstly in the West End of London and later with the Royal Shakespeare Company in Stratford. A few years ago I was sitting waiting for something wonderful to happen, as actors do, when I received a call from a friend who was a newscaster with Sky News. She asked me whether I knew someone who could help a friend of hers who desperately wanted to be a newscaster but had, at that time, a very squeaky, high-pitched voice. I said I'd try to think of someone, but maybe I'd help her myself. 'Give me a few days to think about it,' I said. Two days later, I got a call from the head of Sky News, asking me if I could meet him and discuss the possibility of training around 30 of his reporters whom he felt could do with a little help with their 'on air delivery'.

Sky News is a 24-hour news station. Nearly everyone has to be able to 'voice' stories or appear on screen. But there was one small problem: I had no plans to teach. I was an actor who wanted to direct actors!

Nevertheless I went to meet the man and walked out 90 minutes later, having agreed to start the following week. I returned home to think about what I was going to do with them! Like driving a car, I'd forgotten how I did what I did. Somehow, I was going to have to remember, over the next few days, what I'd taken for granted for over 20 years. But was my way of approaching a text any use to a newscaster? After all, they can't get emotional, they can't allow the story to actually touch them. Their job is to be dispassionate. Isn't it?

My own training as an actor had taken three years, exploring every aspect of voice, movement, the understanding of text, the history of drama and its context within our society. It also included a lot of acting! Now, acting is about finding the emotional truth of the words you're saying. It's not about hiding. It demands an honesty of emotion, which I found truly scary when I first began my course at the age of 19. I did all I could to cling on to my emotional shield. I was frightened that the real me was boring and dull and pathetic. I'd imagined acting would let me hide behind the characters I played, to build a bigger and better shield! I found instead I had to face my fears and show the very private and frightened part of me I'd hoped to hide. Yet when I finally did drop my mask, the world didn't laugh and jeer. With the support of someone else's words I finally risked it. Their words gave me the means of expressing what had been trapped inside me for so many years. My sense of relief was wonderful. My feeling of elation was incredible. I felt as though I could now do anything!

How was I going to find a way of condensing those three years into a matter of hours for journalists who would probably be somewhat sceptical of an actor's ability to teach them how to read the news?!

I've now trained hundreds of newscasters, presenters, people in business and public figures. What's become clear is that virtually everything I do as an actor is exactly what anyone who needs to speak to others and really reach their 'audience' must learn to do. For, in essence, an actor's training teaches you to break through your barrier of fear and be honest about what you really feel. It's not a training to lie, but to speak truthfully, from the heart. To share a part of yourself, just as you would if you were talking to your best and dearest friend. By finding your true voice, you discover a sense of relief and release which transforms every part of your life. If you dare to risk it, you can talk to anyone!

I've written many speeches for some of my clients, helping them express what they really wanted to say. I only achieved this by listening to that part of them which they'd always tried to keep hidden. The speeches were written through them and for them. And yes, a part of me was in there too. Because when we speak honestly, without evasion, using our true voice, we touch that part of each and every person who hears us which is common to us all. Anyone who's listening will be moved by what we say. But when we hide behind a shield of fear, the voice we use belongs to us alone. And, sadly, for many it's a very lonely voice.

In all our lives we've had moments when we've been able to talk to someone honestly and openly and felt safe to use our very private voice. Not so long ago, a friend of mine knocked on my door unexpectedly. He'd just returned from the funeral of a woman he used to do odd jobs for when he was a boy. They'd become friends, but he hadn't seen her to speak to for a number of years. Some months before we'd talked about how wonderful it would be for him to see her again. She held a special place in his past, which I felt he needed to return to, as he was now feeling very confused as to where his true direction lay. She was a marker to a part of him that he'd lost.

He didn't go and see her. She died without them speaking again. As he stood there, I asked what he'd like to say to her if she were here now. He started to cry very softly while he told me (and her) what he felt about their friendship: how important she'd been to him as he'd made his transition from a boy into a young man; how she'd treated him as a person, not just as a son or pupil.

As he spoke, his tears didn't make me feel sad. I felt elated. As he spoke, he showed me the genuineness of his feelings. He was showing me a side of him that I knew was there, but which he'd always felt he had to keep hidden – hidden behind a mask of brash confidence, which at best amused and at worst angered and irritated. For the first time he'd come out of hiding. The man who was now speaking to me was the man I'd hoped to reach when we first met. He hadn't lost any of his strength. He hadn't lost any of his belief in himself nor had he gone down in my estimation as a human being. In fact he'd grown – grown into himself. He'd allowed me to hear, for the first time, his true voice. And it was wonderful.

What I've just described is a very intimate moment in someone's life. He was exposed and vulnerable, but felt safe and secure in our friendship to show me his true feelings. His honesty and integrity reached out to me, filling me with a feeling of being treated with total respect as a listener. Though I said virtually nothing, I was included in a very real and genuine conversation which we both shared. It belonged to us both.

It isn't every day that you'll feel safe enough to open yourself in the way my friend did, but perhaps during the course of this book you'll come to understand that speaking openly and honestly from the heart is what communication, the 'perfect conversation', is really all about. I'm not going to teach you how to fake what you feel or hoodwink anyone into believing what you don't believe yourself! What I will do is to help you to become empowered by finding your true voice, expressing yourself more fully and completely than ever before.

CHAPTER ONE

AIMS

This book's sole intention is to help you to talk more honestly and openly, without fear – whether one to one, to a handful at a meeting, to thousands at a conference or to millions through radio and television.

By exploring the two most important aspects of talking – the voice you use to communicate and how to prepare yourself emotionally – I'll help you to recreate the qualities of a perfect conversation every time you speak.

Your voice is an instrument to be played. If it's not working well and up to the demands placed on it when you get up talk, how can you ever hope to be truly heard? How can you ever hope to express what you really feel if your instrument lets you down?

Emotional preparation is also essential. So many people are afraid to face their fear of speaking to others. The fear of fear can all too easily swamp them when they start to talk. How they deal with this drop-dead gut-wrenching fear varies from trying to keep control of their emotions by hiding behind a mask or by asking the listener to forgive them for not being very good! Neither approach ever allows them to speak with any conviction or passion. We all have to learn, but in no other area of life do we assume we can just do it, without properly preparing ourselves! We wouldn't let someone fly a jumbo jet with 500 people on board who'd only ever flown a toy glider, for example! Yet strangely we assume anyone should be able to get up and talk without any proper help.

In the time I've been involved in helping people to talk, I've realized how confused most people are as to what communication is all about. Somehow, the basic reason for talking to another person – to communicate your thoughts and to tell your story, whatever it is, as truthfully and as honestly as you can – has got lost. The whole world over loves to be told stories. True stories or ones we know have been made up, we really don't mind, so long as they contain emotional truth. The story-teller has to be touched by the story. And for that, they first have to understand themselves! The most important part of a drama training is to appreciate the purpose and need that we all have to tell and be told stories. The performer has to accept they're the messenger of the story. They have to face up to their fears and learn to use the amazing surge of energy that's being given to them when they stand in front of a group of people. And finally they have to prepare their bodies and voices to express their emotions through their words, as fully and as clearly as possible.

Every human being who dares to stand up in front of people and speak has an enormous responsibility to talk from the heart. That's what you and I are going to explore together.

Talking to people is always emotional, there's no getting away from it, but learning how to express yourself honestly won't be as scary or as difficult as you imagine. I'll also take you to find your true voice – the one you always knew was there, but were too afraid to use. I'll explore with you the qualities of a perfect conversation and show you how to achieve it every time you speak.

I'll be using aspects of my own training and experience as an actor and draw on what I've learned from working with people who are learning to communicate. My drama training took three years. Time after time I felt as if I couldn't deal with being so vulnerable. I wanted to go back behind my screen and hide. I wanted to quit. Yet I knew if I didn't face my fear I'd be lost. When I did finally break through, my newfound ability to express my emotions suddenly made sense of my life. But you don't need to be an actor to experience that feeling, nor will it take you three years!

Fear is the key that locks the door on everyone's potential. If you feel safe to speak, your natural honesty and eloquence will be heard. I hope to take you to face your fear and demystify what it is that makes some people terrible speakers and others brilliant. My intention is to help you be one of the latter! As we explore how to find the key to unlock that hidden part of you, the rest will surely follow, giving you the confidence to show your true self more and more of the time.

The confidence to speak easily to an audience of 3,000 people, believe it or not, is already in you. But what you possibly need most of all is the *belief* that it's there. It will grow, as we explore both physically and emotionally the things that stop you.

In addition, we'll contemplate what sound really is, the energy involved and its power and effect. We'll look at the origins of language and our need as humans to communicate. We'll look at the ritual we enter into with the people we speak to.

We'll explore and develop your own power to create sound and the effect it has on your whole being, as well as on others. We'll examine the links between words and emotion and the effect all words have on you, even as you say them. Also, how the physical act of speaking words will help you to get in touch with your own feelings and your own power. We'll look at what fear really is and how you can turn it into something wonderfully powerful and positive. Really!

We'll look at different methods you can use to develop your ability to relax in readiness for speaking under stress. We'll strengthen your vocal muscles and increase your breath power, enabling you to express virtually anything you want to say, in whatever way you want to say it.

We'll explore the qualities that make for the perfect conversation and develop a way for you to recreate them every time you speak. We'll survey some of the many situations you may find yourself in when you need or have to talk, and find practical ways to deal with them as they arise, whether it be talking to a child or talking to your boss (well, yes, maybe it's the same thing!) We'll look at the practical preparations necessary to speak to groups of people, either large or small, including speaking to a conference of thousands.

We'll go through step by step what you'll need to do if you ever have to prepare for a major speech, right up to and including your delivery.

That should be enough to be going on with!

Speaking to other people can be anything from a pleasure to a nightmare. However good or bad you believe you are at communicating your thoughts and dreams to the world around you, I know that by understanding and experiencing what we're going to do together, your ability will grow more than you ever imagined. All I ask in return is for you occasionally to put your brain in neutral and trust your guts. Allow yourself to explore your potential in a different way. Give your imagination the chance to run free and find an alternative route – after all, what you've tried in the past didn't work. Most of all I need you to give yourself the present of a little time.

You already know you have the potential to talk to people in a different and more complete way. All I'm going to do is help you rediscover how to achieve it. But you're the one who's going to make the changes. You're the one who's going to let it happen, with just a little help from me. By taking responsibility for making those changes yourself, you're already further down the line of your own success than most people have ever dared to go.

But first I want you to understand why it is that it hasn't worked for you in the past by reliving the story of how you arrived at this point in your life. Only then, with a whole new understanding of your past, will you be able to unlock your future full potential. Only then will the practical exercises that come later in the book have any real meaning. Only then will you be able to be brilliant! So please, don't rush it. Please give yourself the time to absorb this first part of the book.

MAKING A TAPE

I'd like you, if you would, to make a tape of yourself, either using video or sound. I'd like you to talk about what matters to you: what makes you happy, what makes you sad; what angers you, what excites you. Talk about people you like and why you like them. Talk about those you don't like and why. If you've got someone who can ask the questions for you, great. If not, make a list of questions you'd like to ask yourself. Have a go.

I want you to remember that it's not intended to be a performance, nor a judgement on you. Nor a great piece of television or radio, so please don't perform! See whether you can go beyond your initial embarrassment and keep going until you forget about the fact that you're recording.

This tape is a way of you seeing and hearing yourself now. If you don't want to look or listen to it for a while, don't. When you do, I want you to look and listen *behind* all those bits that make you squirm. Be kind to yourself. There'll be a person who, despite all the embarrassment and 'um's and 'ah's, is actually very lovable. You'll start to see the person your close friends see and hear. Because I assure you they know you better than you imagine.

While you're thinking about it, let's begin to look at sound – if that's not a contradiction in terms!

CHAPTER TWO

THE POWER OF SOUND

SO WHAT IS SOUND?

When you talk, you're using one of the most powerful forms of energy there is. The words you use are only part of the story. The words are formed out of sound.

Pause for a moment and just listen. Listen to the sounds around you. Perhaps you're lucky enough to be sitting in the quiet tranquillity of a country garden. The sounds you're hearing are of birds singing, bees buzzing, the wind gently rustling the leaves of a tree. Maybe not! Maybe you're being bombarded by the sounds of traffic screeching, horns sounding off, doors banging. Perhaps you're somewhere in between? How many different sounds can you hear? How do they make you feel?

Wherever you are, every sound you're hearing (and even those you can't) is having an effect on your whole body right now. Every single sound is affecting your mood and your well-being. Some of the sounds stress you out and make you feel tense and irritable. Others help to release the tension in your body, bringing you ever nearer to contentment, bringing you back into harmony with your life. You're surrounded by a sea of sound every minute of every day. Everything's in motion, from the movement of the sea to the shifting of continents. Even in the most silent places on the planet there'll be sound. And even when you're being really quiet, you'll still be adding to the sounds around you. Haven't you ever tried to get to sleep and heard the pulse in your head pushing against your pillow?

IN THE BEGINNING

Let's go back in time, say between eight and fourteen thousand million years! According to current scientific knowledge this was the moment of the 'Big Bang', when the universe as we know it began. At the very moment before it happened, all 'matter' was compressed into a mass of unbelievable density. With the explosion, the matter expanded away from the centre with a ferocious force pushing it out into the void. As matter and energy bombarded together and started to slow, the galaxies, stars and the planets of our universe began to form. Every particle in the universe, including those in your own body, was present in that moment. Incredible, isn't it? Keeps me awake at night, too!

Physics tells us that matter is made up of molecules, which are made up of atoms, which are made up of protons, neutrons and electrons, which are made up of quarks. And quarks are not matter at all, but the smallest known form of pure energy! So everything we consider to be solid isn't solid at all! It's pure energy, organized in a particular form. Each particle within each molecule, within each piece of matter is moving and vibrating in a particular way at a particular speed. Which means to say, the room you're in, the chair you're sitting on, the book you're holding, aren't solid at all. They're organized, vibrating energy. So are you! All energy is in constant motion, creating the world we all know and love! Nothing is static, nothing is still, yet everything is always striving to find a level of vibration in harmony with the energy around it.

Another thing worth mentioning is that matter can neither be created or destroyed – which isn't to say that the organization of that energy can't change! And if and when it does, the excess energy has to go somewhere. It doesn't just disappear!

Sound is the result of a release of energy. So now let's explore, in terms of energy, what happens leading up to you hitting a bell. Energy from the sun in the form of heat and light is turned by plants into energy which you eat directly, or indirectly via another animal. Your body turns this into energy which your muscles then turn into action when you hit the bell. The energy of the sun is turned into motion.

The bell, before you hit it, is quiet, in its natural state of equilibrium. All the molecules in the bell have their place, but the bell gently wobbles with the movement of the particles of energy which make up the molecules. It's very quietly ringing!

Then you hit the bell! The molecules at the point of impact take the full force. One strike won't persuade them to disconnect from each other (unless there's enough energy to smash the bell). So they start to wobble really quickly. But they can't move much, except to bump into the molecules around them, which in turn bump into those around *them*. The energy starts to move away from the point of impact in all directions in a wave, just like the waves created by a stone being dropped into a pond, but in all possible directions.

When these waves of energy reach the furthest points from the impact, most of the energy starts coming back to the source. This wave of energy continues to move through the bell, causing all the molecules in it to vibrate. The whole bell is now 'wobbling' much faster than it was before you hit it!

The rate of 'wobble' is defined by how many molecules make up the bell. Big bells have more molecules than little bells, so the waves of energy take longer to reach all of the molecules. The longer it takes, the deeper the note. So little bells have higher notes than big bells. How loud the bell is depends on how fast the molecules are wobbling, which depends on how much energy was sent into the bell when you hit it. If you hit it really hard the molecules in the bell will wobble much more than if you hit it softly. So, the bigger the bell, the deeper the note. The harder the hit, the bigger the wobble, the louder the note.

There is, however, an escape route, enabling the molecules and the bell to return to their state of equilibrium and quieten down. The molecules on the surface of the bell bump into the molecules of air surrounding the bell. These in turn bump into the molecules surrounding them, transferring the energy away from the bell in all directions. This creates waves of pressure – air pressure. The air bumps molecule on molecule, until molecules of air in your ear bump the surface of your eardrum, setting up a wobble (a copy of the bell's wobble), which impacts on the nerves. They, in turn, pass the energy to the brain, which checks out the sound with anything it has heard in the past. 'I know that sound. It's a bell!'

What about when you put your fingers in your ears? You can still hear the bell, as the sound vibrates the molecules in your fingers too and reaches the eardrum through them. It's the difference between blowing out a candle a few feet away and shouting at it! When you blow, you set up a stream of air molecules and after you've pushed the molecules of air out of the way, the air in your lungs will eventually reach the candle. If you shout, 'Go out!', the candle will probably stay alight, but someone in the next room might jump! As we all know, sound energy is transferred through walls too!

The human ear can detect a change in the pressure on the eardrum of one ten millionth of one per cent. It really can hear a pin drop a long way off. The only thing that stops us hearing something so small is the other sounds which swamp it out. Across a busy city street it's unlikely you'll hear the pin hit the ground!

The movement of air by the wind will also take a sound away. The molecules in the air which are vibrating with sound energy are literally blown away. Remember how on a still summer's day a single voice can be heard over vast distances and on a windy day the sound of a voice can be lost?

Let's go back to the bell. Believe it or not, you have certain things in common. You are somewhat more complicated, in that you have a multitude of molecules of different kinds, yet every particle in every molecule that makes up the cells of your body – the organs, the bones, the muscles, the skin and your brain – vibrates at different frequencies – on different notes. Your whole body is a complex web of organized energy, working and vibrating in harmony. Like a very complex chord of musical sound, each different note, from each part of your body, each vibration, makes up your 'body sound'. At any given time, you're sending out a chord of sound which is an expression of your-self, even when you're not talking!

Your body, like the bell, is always trying to get back into its ideal state of harmony and equilibrium, for the sake of each individual molecule and for the sake of your whole being, releasing energy back out it doesn't want to hold on to.

When it's out of harmony with itself your body sound changes and other people hear it! Not just through their ears, but through their bodies. Haven't you ever experienced meeting someone and feeling they gave off 'bad vibes'? Even before they spoke or even looked at you, you felt uncomfortable, unsettled? Remember visiting friends who've just had a row. You can feel the energy as you walk through the door!

Your emotional and physical state is always affecting your 'body sound'. When you talk, the tone of your voice will be an expression of that sound. Of course, everyone's ideal 'sound' is different, depending on their shape and size. If your body's in harmony and working well, you'll be speaking with a tone of voice which is a reflec-tion of your ideal state, in harmony with your 'body sound'. But if your body's not in harmony, your voice will reflect that too! It's almost as if the sounds of the words contain all the frequencies, from all the parts of your body, which are in a state of dis-ease. You can hear it echoed in the tones you use.

Your state of harmony is affected by the sounds received by your ears and on into your brain. Yet your whole body is a receptor for sound. You're affected not just through your ears, but also directly into your body. Some of this sound you're aware of and some you're not. Every sound that reaches you affects every single cell in your body, either directly or indirectly, either positively or negatively.

A friend of mine is totally deaf. When we went to a firework display she had a great time watching the fireworks, but she was also thrilled by the ones she could feel through her body! Another example of how sound can affect your body positively is the use of ultrasound to heal damaged muscles by sending waves of sound at a frequency which reharmonizes the unhealthy molecules. Ultrasound can also be used to smash kidney stones by sending sound to them at a frequency which causes the molecules in the stones to vibrate so fast that they break apart. Even the human voice is capable of doing this with a crystal glass. Not that I'm going to suggest smashing things up with your voice – but you could!

So sound affects every aspect of your life: some sounds affect you positively, by bringing you back into harmony; others stress you out by creating a disharmony in the whole, or part, of you.

Think what people's voices can do to your state of well-being. For example, the actor Anthony Hopkins could read the phone book and you'd feel good just listening. Yet someone with a high-pitched squeal could send you running from the room!

Think what your voice can do to other people. Think what your voice does to you! The sound you make reinforces how you feel about yourself every time you speak, for good or ill!

Listen again to the sounds around you. Focus on them. Do you like them? Do they make you feel well?

All of us are points on the fantastic web of organized vibrating energy that touches the farthest reaches of the universe, a universe still striving to achieve its own state of harmony and equilibrium. At all times, your point on the web is being affected by outside sources. But you're not just a passive receiver: you're a part of the sound. You're an active participator, affecting the ebb and flow of the world you live in with the sounds that you make. And one of the most powerful ways you affect the environment you live in is your use of sound in language. But where did language come from?

A Brief History of Language

When humans first walked the Earth, their ability to communicate with each other was somewhat limited! Before they had language, they used body gestures and sound, as do all animals, to help them survive – to help them re-establish their 'natural state of harmony and equilibrium'.

Let's imagine you have a pet dog called George. When George sees you, he wags his tail and makes a high-pitched squeal or maybe barks. You say, 'Hello, George,' in a warm friendly tone. Maybe he tries to lick your face and jump up, expressing his pleasure at seeing and hearing you. There's an emotional release of energy. He goes from a state of low energy to high. George releases the energy he's held in store and returns himself to a state of happy harmony – you're home!

When he's hungry, he'll let you know by going to where the food is and whining or maybe barking at you while wagging his tail. If he's finally managed to get you to feed him and you decide to take his bowl away before he's finished, you might well get a growl of dissatisfaction. If you happen to tread on his tail, he'll let out a yelp. First he releases the energy that's come into him – your foot squashing his tail – and second, by sending the energy back out in the form of sound, you hear the wave of pain in his voice and move your foot!

All the sounds and body gestures George makes are either a release of vocal and physical energy or an expression of 'disharmony' which helps to bring him back into equilibrium. All of which helps him survive!

For millions of years we humans managed quite well, just like George, getting what we needed without the use of words. Our needs were very simple: food, warmth and a little love and affection to help produce the next generation! But as human existence became more complex, we had to find a more precise way of expressing our needs in order to sustain our state of harmony and survive. As the family groups became larger, the well-being of an individual became more and more dependent on the well-being of the whole family. It was necessary to help each individual, as well as the whole group, to understand what was necessary for everyone to survive.

So over hundreds of thousands of years we developed the ability to create more and more complex sounds. We developed our lung power to change the tones and sounds we were able to make. As our needs grew, we expressed more and more accurately what we wanted to communicate to bring us and our group back into harmony.

As time went on we developed more powerful lips and tongue muscles to reflect even more accurately what we wanted to express. The sounds we made developed into our first simple words – a series of sounds which communicated even more precisely what we wanted or needed. First came the need, then a movement or gesture, then a sound and finally a word.

As family groups turned into tribes, these simple words had to express more and more information. Language developed to handle the increased amount of information which needed to be shared between the members of a tribe. Their continued survival and well-being depended on it!

As the tribal groups grew ever larger, so too did the number of words needed to sustain them. No longer was it possible to survive with just a few simple words and gestures. The same basic human needs required not only sounds, but an ever more sophisticated language to achieve the same results – a state of equilibrium and harmony for the individual and for the whole group.

Let's imagine we're part of the tribe called 'Vara', living thousands of years ago. We have advanced to a stage where language has developed sufficiently for us to have a word for everything around us. We grow our own food. We fish and hunt. When the food is plentiful we sing with the sheer pleasure of living. Our tribal elders are truly wise. Our medicine men bring our bodies back into harmony and our shamans help us to communicate and stay in harmony with the gods when our spirits are unwell.

Sounds and words are a crucial part of our tribal life. If we have a shortage of food, the elders will talk to the whole tribe. Each person is allowed to speak and be heard. The words are always carefully chosen to explain what is needed to change the course of events.

Our shamans and medicine men always remind us of the power of the gods and how we need to respect the energies we're a part of and to always try to be in harmony with the Earth and the heavens.

The history of the tribe is always remembered by the elders. We journey back in time through our stories. The myths and legends of our tribe are re-enacted to us with great passion and drama to remind our hearts as well as our heads of the great truths we need to hear and feel again and again. They give us an understanding of our present lives, through our past. This is how we reharmonize the spirits and bodies of each member of the tribe.

We know the importance of allowing the tribe to express itself as a whole. We share in the making of sound through chanting and singing and dancing to bring about a change in the energy of the tribe and of the gods. By sharing these sounds and words, we share in each other's energy. Sharing our energy strengthens our community. When the tribe is in harmony through sound and words, each of us is moved to a feeling of well-being. Sound redirects the energy of the tribe. It makes us well again. It raises our spirits and calms our fears. It brings the tribe back into harmony for the greater good. It helps us survive.

Just as sound can bring our own bodies back into harmony, so too can it bring a whole group back into harmony. All are organized energy systems, all need to be in harmony to function well. So sound played an ever-increasing role in the rituals of tribal life to improve the well-being of the community. Just like ultrasound on a knee, sounds and words carried the energy needed to bring both the individual and the tribe back into harmony through the frequency of the tones, the frequency of the rhythms and the rhythms and tones of each individual word. The number and types of rituals used by any given tribe expressed their group personality, their group rhythm, dynamically different from the neighbouring tribes yet interconnected, part of an even greater harmony of sound by which they all were joined.

For thousands and thousands of years, nothing has changed, only the scale. Now we live in communities of millions, yet our individual tribes are likely to be found in our personal address books. Our village is likely to be where we work. The elders are the government of the day or the heads of multinational corporations, our shamans have divided into priests and actors, our medicine men into doctors, psychotherapists, homoeopaths, reflexologists, and so on. But our basic needs are still the same – the simple need to release energy through sound to bring both the individual and the tribe back into harmony continues to this day.

The only problem is that many modern day 'tribes' have lost touch with what that natural state really is! More often than not it's left to individuals to try and bring themselves back into harmony. Every weekend we leave our cities to 'get away' to find some peace and quiet. We use our CD players to make the sounds and words we need to hear. We watch chat shows on television instead of talking to people! We rely more and more on others to give us our feeling of well-being as we lose touch with our own ability to create and share sound with those around us. Yet every time we stop to talk, to exchange our sound with another human being, we give ourselves the chance to bring us both back into harmony by exchanging emotion through words.

WORDS AND EMOTION

Words came out of sounds, which came out of gestures, which came out of a release of energy, which came out of a need to be in harmony in order to survive, as we've just seen.

Each word we use has its own history, its own, almost hidden code to effect a release of energy which comes from our most basic need to survive. Most of us take the words we use for granted, oblivious of the power they have on us and those we speak to. But every time you say a word you affect the emotional state of both the person listening and yourself.

Take, for instance, someone saying, 'Don't!' What you hear first is the emotional intensity behind the word, which, in its simplest form, could be either a warning or a plea, affecting either your or the speaker's survival. It will be an expression of their disharmony, their fear, expressed by using exactly the same tones as our ancestors. The level of disharmony will be contained in the tones they use. This is what you hear first. Then you hear the sounds that make up the word: D.O.N.T. We compare this complex code of tones and sounds, a beat after the emotional sound, with what that particular combination means to us. First we hear the emotion which triggered the word and then we break it down into its parts to draw out its particular meaning. We hear and feel the energy before we hear the detail.

Every word was created out of sounds which contain an emotional need to aid the survival of an individual or group. Your ability to connect a word to an emotion is learnt.

Every single word you use has its own history. Most have been handed on over generations, each one passed on from one person to another, a little container of energy, still holding its emotional coded message from the past.

However, words alone can't express precisely what we feel: the tones and sounds and body gestures we use express the true emotion behind the word. 'There, there, it s all right', for example, can either be said with gentle tones to calm someone down or quicker, sharper tones to get their energy mo ring again. The spoken word always contains three elements – the body, the tone and the word itself. All play their part in helping us to really 'hear' the needs of another human being, to understand and experience what they really feel.

If you listen to someone talking in a foreign language, for instance, you can very often tell what they're feeling without understanding a single word! But if you want to know more detail you'll need to know the words. Words are there to help us be more specific about our need. This ability to communicate through language supposedly sets us apart from animals. It gives us the ability to say exactly what we want to say, to express exactly what we really feel. Yet all too often, the true emotion that lies behind someone's words can feel hidden. We no longer clearly hear the original sound, nor, frequently, are we meant to! Yet however sophisticated the words we choose to use, the original sounds and gestures will still be there. Hidden maybe and contained, but still there, still trying to achieve the same results – to return us to a state of equilibrium, harmony and well-being.

Underlying every word we use, the original emotional needs can still be heard. 'How are you today?' can be expressed in a million different ways. So too can the word 'fine'. It really is true – 'It's not what you say, it's how you say it!'

Yet few of us can genuinely say that what comes out of our mouths always expresses what we really feel, nor is it heard exactly as we'd wish. Why not? What goes wrong? Why don't people really hear us? Why can't we just get up and talk without fear, confident that we'll be able to express ourselves fully and clearly, knowing that we'll truly be understood?

If we want to understand why it goes a bit haywire, perhaps we need to go back to what we are in our simplest form: an organized energy system striving to be in harmony!

CHAPTER THREE

GOING WITHIN

THE EMOTIONAL JOURNEY

Energy takes many forms. Love is energy. So too is hate, so too is compassion and so too is fear. All of them are expressions of complex vibrating energy that move in and out and through you. These energies, as they come into you and as you release them back out, change your whole body's state of harmony and well-being and that of those around you. Like all forms of energy, they change the vibrational speed of the molecules in your body. This movement of energy has an immediate effect on you, changing your emotional state. If you choose to try and hold on to energy when you're already vibrating too fast or you release energy when your own is too slow, you can, over time, harm particular organs and tissues in your body, or even damage your whole being.

If you're at all aware of your body's natural state, you have choices. You can return yourself into balance by taking control of the energy, rather than being tossed around by it. When it's moving too fast, you find ways to slow it down. When it's moving too slowly, you try to speed it up. If you're bombarded by outside energy and fail to release it back out, however, you can all too easily start to lose touch with what it feels like to be in harmony. All you know is you feel stressed or unwell. You'll probably try and convince yourself that that's who you are – a naturally over-energized, stressed human being!

When your body's in harmony, as already mentioned, the tone of your voice and the sound that you make when you speak to another human being will be in perfect harmony with your own 'body sound'. Every time you speak the tone of your voice will be an expression of your whole being. You'll know that you're truly being heard. This 'body tone' is unique to you and always in harmony with your 'body sound'. But what if your body is in a state of 'dis-harmony'?

Let's imagine you're planning a touring holiday in your car. You've got all the maps and books recommending wonderful places to visit. You've got your good food guide and your good hotel guide. You're all set, but you've forgotten one thing: the car's not working properly and is making the most dreadful noise. You know something's wrong, but haven't bothered to have it fixed. Wherever you go, whatever you do on your journey, you'll be continuously reminded that the car's not happy. Wherever you are, however beautiful the view, however nice the people you meet on the way, you'll always be hearing the state of the car. The noise will get louder, the car will drive more and more erratically, until eventually you'll start getting so upset that your concentration goes and you'll start taking the wrong turnings and get lost! Every time you stop to talk to someone to ask the way, the sound of the car will distract them. They won't really hear you and will send you off in the wrong direction and you'll get even more lost. Finally the car may pack up while you're trying to get up an impossibly steep hill you never intended to be on in the first place. Your magic journey becomes a nightmare!

Pernaps you ought to have the car serviced right away! Find out what's not working and why and get it sorted before you begin this new journey. (Adding soundproofing to stifle the noise isn't going to be the answer!)

If you, as a person, aren't 'running' properly, the 'noise' you make every time you open your mouth will be telling the world that something's wrong. The way you move and talk and sound will be telling every person you meet on your journey through life that something needs to be fixed. Pretending there isn't a problem just doesn't work! Whatever you try to do to disguise this lack of harmony and well-being, it will always be heard – unless the other person's car is a mess too! Also, your 'dis-harmony' will add to all your listeners' own confusion and discomfort. This vicious circle will continue until you find the true sound of your body and use it every time you speak.

We're all trying to find our place of perfect harmony within the world we live in, but it can't be found if we've lost touch with our own natural state of harmony and equilibrium, however hard we search!

So let's now talk about how energy has affected your equilibrium, your natural state of harmony, well-being and happiness, from the time you were born.

THE EARLY YEARS

Before the momentous moment of your birth, you spent around nine months in a pretty natural state of contentment. Your mother's womb gave you everything you needed. If you weren't happy, you moved around to bring yourself back into harmony. Ask any mother how, in the last few months of pregnancy, her baby thrashed around inside her womb when it wasn't comfortable!

Then you were born – with the perfect means for achieving the perfect state. If you needed to regain your natural state of harmony and equilibrium, you were able to express yourself through sound and body movements. As a baby, you had no problem finding the right note or type of sound or visual clue to express your needs. You could shout and scream or make any manner of sound to get what you needed to bring yourself back into harmony. You didn't get nervous, you didn't think, 'Is it OK for me to make these sounds?' You just made them! That need to express and 'rebalance' your energy by using sound and words continues throughout your life, but, as you'll soon realize, it doesn't always happen the way it should.

Your needs may have been for food or warmth, or to be held. Yet you were able to 'ask' for this 'energy' and you'd usually be heard.

You also needed the energy given by the sound of your parents' voices, especially your mother's. After all, you heard and felt her voice from inside the womb, along with all the other sounds! The rhythm and tones of her voice had the power to reharmonize you and bring you back into a state of equilibrium.

It may have taken your parents a little time to understand your messages, but they were truly 'heard' and understood quite quickly! Your mother was so attuned to you, she could even recognize your cry across a crowded room. She could hear you above almost anything! By hearing your call and by listening carefully, she was able to communicate with you through her sound and her body.

The sounds and tones and body messages you exchanged with your parents bonded you together. Within those first few weeks of life, you'd also have been aware of how in harmony your parents were with each other. It doesn't mean to say their tones would be the same, but ideally they'd be in harmony. Any disharmony in their sounds and rhythms would have been felt by you and you'd have expressed your discomfort in the form of sound.

Hopefully, in the early months, your parents took their lead from you. Initially they adapted to your tones, calming and comforting you with their voices, smiling and grinning almost incessantly! (Which, incidentally, affected the tone of their voices.) They communicated with you on every level; energy flowed freely between you all, constantly returning you to your natural state of equilibrium, both physically and emotionally. You felt secure, sharing with your parents the sounds of contentment, enjoying the pleasure of making sounds for sound's sake. These sounds and rhythms became your markers to what home and safety and love really meant.

Well, ideally!

The golden age of attention all too quickly passes. It cannot be sustained. For the first few years of your life, the family is where you first realize that your own equilibrium is affected by the world around you. The rhythms and sounds and words of your family are what you assume the world to be. You like and need to be in harmony with them. You want to belong and be a part of that feeling. But how?

You start working fast to learn the ropes. You do it by becoming wonderful mimics of your parents. You copy everything. After all, they're your 'role models'. You start to take on their facial mannerisms, the way they stand, the way they move, the way they breathe, the way they make sounds and words. By copying your parents, you're searching for the best way of being in tune with them, as they were with you. You are still trying to keep in touch with your own state of equilibrium, while finding where to fit in with the whole 'chamber orchestra' of your family.

You may not be the first or the last child your parents have. Problems can arise if there are new additions. You may well keep moving around the orchestra until you find a place that works for you and for them – even having to change instrument! For the family to function well, each individual needs to be in harmony with themselves and with those around them. If any family member is not in their ideal place, playing their ideal instrument, their ideal notes, everyone is affected. However, there are good and not so good orchestras! It can be hard to hold the tune if those around you don't know what they're playing! Discord and disharmony result. No music will be played worth listening to!

Of course there are always times of disharmony! A parent telling you off or smacking you can make you feel your world is falling apart. You'll scream and cry to release the vocal or physical energy that's entered your body. It has to be released in some form in order for you to feel better. Hit the bell and the energy comes back out – though not always with a nice tone! But hopefully, all through your childhood you were able to release energy which was hurting you and to receive energy back, in the form of love and affection, when it was needed.

Energy comes into every family from the larger world in many forms, both affecting the equilibrium of the individual and the whole. If the family's working well, it'll always be able to bring itself back into harmony. How well you dealt with it depends on how well your parents were able to deal with it!

What happened when a stranger came into your home with their different energy and sound and rhythm? You'd have naturally felt uncomfortable. Were your parents relaxed and easy or did they tense up and make you feel even more nervous? If, from when you were born, your parents found it easy to adjust, all well and good. If not, you'd have been given a double dose of discomfort: first the visitor's energy shook up your molecules and then you sensed your parents were shaken up too. Scary!

One of the most difficult things for a child to deal with is when a parent brings into the home another sound, another rhythm from, say, their place of work. As a young child you can feel very upset that the family's sound has been changed. If a parent comes home in a bad mood, the very difference from the normal energy in the home changes your own rhythm. This can be frightening and make you feel very unsafe. You don't know what this energy is and you don't like the feeling. So you try to change the rhythm, the tone, to get yourself back into harmony. You'll do almost anything! Yet at three or four years old you won't necessarily know how to achieve it!

This anxiety, this energy, needs to be released. It needs to be expressed. It needs to be heard. The parent needs to explain so the child understands why the energy's changed and knows it's not their fault. But what if a parent isn't too good at coming in and saying, 'I've had a terrible day at work. It's not your fault I'm in a bad mood. Let me express this energy that's upsetting me and turn it into something more positive'? Well, something like that!

The energy really can be transformed by talking it out. If a family is able to appreciate how important it is to work together to release any 'bad vibes', it will help each member to get back in touch with their own state of harmony. Doesn't always happen though, does it?

If the talking isn't done, the wave of energy which comes into the home still has to be dealt with. So the child will resort to any 'family survival strategies' they've learnt from their parents to release the energy again. What are these strategies? Whenever energy which frightens a particular family comes in, the family members will send out a call for their 'energy survival pack'. The messenger they send is known as 'adrenalin'. This triggers a massive release of stored energy into their bodies to either fight off the danger or to run away. This state of energy overload is known as 'fight or flight'. What a family decides to do depends on its strategies – what it believes has helped it survive in the past.

In the 'fight' mode, the family members will blow up and get it out of their system. This strategy doesn't immediately help the state of harmony though, even if the parent may initially feel better for shouting at the child! The wave of energy swashes around the home until it's dealt with properly, or it finds some way out of the door, or each individual has to deal with it elsewhere.

There's also 'flight' mode – get away from the energy pronto and disappear, escape from what's not wanted, in the hope that the energy gets dissipated elsewhere! Remember going to your room and hiding until your dad or mum calmed down?

All this assumes the family knows what it means to be in harmony! What if it doesn't? What if the individuals are totally out of balance with themselves? What if their family fears tell them that all energy coming in is a threat to their very survival?

Families who can only ever move into 'fight' mode will express the energy in either physical or verbal violence. Words and sounds are used just like fists to dump the energy onto another member of the family. These families' energies are so out of control they destroy any possibility of harmony. Each member will live their lives surrounded by emotional and possibly physical violence with little hope of finding their natural state of equilibrium.

Families who only ever move into 'flight' mode will always be running away from everyone. Never wanting a confrontation, never wanting to upset anyone, never wanting to risk any real closeness in case they get hurt, they end up running away from their very lives.

However, some families deal with the energy by staying in a limbo state of permanent 'fight or flight'. Neither able to run away or express this 'energy overload', they try to hold the energy deep within themselves. There is no release! The energy is repressed, held within each family member's body, drastically affecting their state of harmony and equilibrium. This too can be another form of violence, not just towards themselves but also towards those around them. Either nothing is given out or what is said and done doesn't have any connection to their true emotional state. This 'held in' energy can destroy the harmony within both individuals and families. All are affected.

A child from a 'blocked' family will try and make sense of what's going on, instinctively knowing it's not right. Such children feel uncomfortable. They want to voice out their pain as they did as a baby. Some will rebel with fits of angry sound to try and 'get it out of their systems'. Others will feel they daren't let it out in the form of sound, so they become physically violent instead. Others try to hold it all in! They lock up their voices, they lock up their bodies. They'll try to stop any emotional release whatsoever in order to stay within the family, to continue to belong. But the energy still needs and tries to come back out. This 'dis-ease' is expressed in many forms. The mildest is when muscles tense up with the excess energy, like a headache. The energy escapes slowly through the surface of the body in the form of heat. The expression 'getting hot under the collar' has more truth than we think!

But if the child continues to try and hide their pain, the energy has no safe way out. Children's small bodies do the best they can to absorb this excess energy and continue to function, until some part of them seizes up. If they're lucky, an opportunity to express their pain, to be heard, is offered when their parents seek help for the child's illness. But if the energy's still not released, it can become so serious that their bodies will at some point pack up all together. Some people call this 'stress-related illness'.

This failure of a family to have a healthy means of expressing these build ups of energy will inevitably take each individual further and further away from their natural state of well-being. The sounds and rhythms they were born with become a distant memory.

More people than maybe we realize live their lives in a state of total disharmony! Yet if we listen carefully, their adult voices will be telling us what lies behind their façade. Children who held their energy in will have a voice which is holding back, keeping a tight lid on their emotions. Those who rebelled will have a harshness in the way they speak, still fighting to be heard. The ones who ran away will hardly be heard or noticed by anyone. Each will have a voice expressing how they really feel. The sounds of discord and disharmony will still be heard in everything they say.

Of course it's not always like this. If you're fortunate, you'll have known moments when your family came together and everyone felt connected, in tune with each other and within themselves. Those are the magic moments we all crave and adore: each person able to sing their own true song, to express all their feelings, both good and bad, freely without being blocked. You are in tune with your orchestra. It makes you feel well.

OFF TO SCHOOL

Let's assume you had some of the good bits going for you. What happens to that state of harmony when you first go to school? With any luck you'll have spent time in other 'worlds' through visits, going shopping and people coming into your home. You'll feel reasonably secure in your own state of equilibrium, safe in your family's rhythm and tone and able to cope with it being disrupted, for you know it will be reharmonized. You'll have enough experience of the outside world and other people's 'orchestras' to know that it's OK to make trips out!

Even so, going to school for the first time is really quite shocking for your organized energy system. You walk into a massive wave of differing energies! Even if you have experienced a gentler level of it in the past, it can be totally overwhelming. You're not used to it staying at such a high level and you don't always know what to do with it.

What's the tempo, what's the tune? It's coming from all directions. It shakes you up, your molecules start racing! 'Where's Mummy? Get me out of here!'

The rhythms of school life are usually faster, the sounds usually louder. There's a mess of energy flying around. That's what big groups do! Our first steps into this new world are crucial. Another family to do it all over again with, but it's so enormous, help! Now, playgroups are a good starter – two hours of big lumps of energy and a feeling of dis-harmony and then we go home, great!

Children adapt, as long as they can get to grips with the rhythm and sounds of the new group, so long as they have regular reminders of home and can touch base with their own tone and 'vibration'! Yet the clash of worlds takes a while to settle down. Each child brings with them to school the rules of the game from home. Each home is different, each set of rules is different. Some find it easy to join this new world, because it's similar to home! Others find it so exciting and invigorating they bring it all home with them and bang, the family, usually the parents, can't deal with it and shut them up! Still others find it difficult to adjust to the sounds out there, so go home and are very quiet or angry. Their energy is being swamped by the excesses at school and they're not being heard. Their own family rhythms and tones don't help them to find their place in the bigger world. Then there are those of course who aren't being heard at home, so take their anger and frustrations to school – the bully, the joker, the know all!

So a whole new balancing act has to take place. It takes very good teachers to recognize the needs of each child as they try to bridge the worlds of school and home. Again, if you're lucky, your teachers will have made it easy for you to integrate your two worlds while still letting you stay in touch with your own natural rhythm and energy. Your voice will have been heard as part of the whole, not excluded or denied, but a unique instrument in the ever-growing orchestra of your life.

All this new energy flying around needs to be released, to be expressed, to be heard. I was visiting a friend recently. As I got out of my car, I heard this incredible noise coming from behind a wall. I realized it was a school playground full of what sounded like screaming kids. As I moved closer, I could hear more of the individual sounds, though I couldn't hear the words. Some children were screaming, some were singing, some were laughing. Others were just talking very loudly. But all of them seemed to be making a heck of a lot of noise.

It was their afternoon break and they'd been sent into the playground to do just that. They were releasing pent up energy by laughing and running and feeling their sound. They were sent to do this three times a day. But they wanted and needed to do it. Most of them loved doing it – talking, laughing, singing, running about; keeping their voices open and free; 'rebalancing' themselves.

Sitting in a classroom learning facts and figures is pretty important for children's long-term well-being. However, it can put them into a state of overload which isn't so helpful to their natural equilibrium!

The overwhelming need to express and rebalance your energy by using sound and words remains with you throughout your life, but fewer and fewer opportunities present themselves for you to do it on a regular basis. Schoolchildren are given permission to be rowdy and loud at least three times a day, but who can say the same as an adult? You may say you don't want or need to do it. Yet how often have you wanted to shout for joy with the sheer pleasure of being alive, but didn't? It wasn't appropriate! Grown ups just don't do that. Really? Vocal and emotional release are just as important for adults. If you want to express yourself more fully when you talk to others, now's the time to begin again to express what you really feel. If you're frightened of scaring the neighbours, do it in the car or into a pillow. Maybe you like to believe you're quite happy only ever expressing yourself with a gentle, quiet voice. You'll be surprised how good it makes you feel to make a lot of sound. You will only find out if you try!

OK, back to school!

School is where you establish many of your first independent long-term relationships. There are hundreds of new beings within the school and, say, 30 in the class, that you have daily, hourly, minute by minute contact with, plus of course the teachers. Meeting them as individuals, experiencing the difference in their energy, is both exciting and frightening. As we've seen, much depends on how you were brought up by your parents to handle this energy. If you were still in touch with your natural state of harmony and well-being, you hopefully found the experience enjoyable. Also, maybe for you, school, more than home, was where you were able to get closer to your natural state of well-being. In the mix of energy, you were able to find one or several friends whose rhythms and tones came close to your own – people who listened and let you talk out your pain, your joys and your excitement, who let you feel comfortable with who you really were. And you were able to do the same for them.

However, school isn't always an easy place to keep in touch with your ideal state of well-being! The stresses take their toll. Not all the children I heard in the playground were necessarily having a great time! Not all of them were equipped to cope with the verbal or physical violence that can be found in any school. For many, the seeds of their disharmony and discontent had already been sown. The rhythm and tones of their family life had already been established. School just made things worse! The children from 'fight' mode families dumped their angry energy into anyone and anything. The 'flight' mode children would try and hide as best they could. Those who were in a permanent state of 'fight or flight' would be frozen with fear most of the time trying to hold it all in, some of them lashing out when it all got too much! And the teachers? They come in all forms too, adding their own personal mixed up energy to the swirl within the school.

The confusion for many of the children trying keep the bridge open between their two worlds was already taking its toll, causing them to close down their free flow of energy and sound. They didn't know what to do for the best. And, what was worse, they didn't feel safe to tell anyone – not their parents, not their teachers, not even their friends. Nobody seemed to notice how badly they were crying out to be heard.

ADOLESCENCE

By adolescence you'll be using all the strategies you've already learnt to help you belong, to cope with the ever-changing energy around you. These may not be the best for keeping you in touch with your own equilibrium, but they've given you the means of staying connected, of belonging, however tenuously, to those around you. As your horizons grow, you begin to be bombarded by what's happening in the world outside your home and school. You become more aware of the massive sea of energy you'll have to come to terms with. You become more aware of sex and the intimacy it will entail. Your whole energy system starts to 'vibrate' so fast, you don't know how to slow it down.

Whatever's going on in your life becomes all the more heightened by all this energy. But what to do with it? The family often can't cope with the deluge flying around the home. So nobody gets heard at all. The orchestra isn't just out of key or in the wrong rhythm, it has more than likely been disbanded! School handles it with varying success. But hundreds of pupils, all going berserk, with so much energy in them, are not easy to deal with, straining the communication skills of all concerned.

As you move through adolescence you continue to search for your place in the world. If you're lucky, you'll have stayed in touch with your state of harmony. You'll have been supported by your family and school life. Somewhere inside you'll know you're still on course. But what if you don't feel connected? What if you don't feel in touch with your equilibrium? Whatever you're feeling, the rush of energy around you and in you can confuse and obscure who and what you really are and where you wish to go. **In your need to belong, finding *a* place in the world can often feel more important than finding *the* place.**

Throughout adolescence the search becomes ever more urgent. Eagerly, you look for new role models. You may well begin to hunt outside school for those you believe have got it right, those who, in some way, express what you're feeling. Those who express what you want to feel! You start to mimic them – pop stars, movie stars, older friends and acquaintances, whoever! In your innocence and ignorance you may well end up being taken further and further away from where you truly belong, swayed by television, advertising, films, books and magazines into believing your natural state of well-being isn't 'it', that people 'out there' have all the answers. You've yet to find out that many of them are speaking to you from a place of total disharmony, which they're desperate for you to join. They want and need you to belong to their madness!

Trying to keep up, trying to belong, you can move further and further from your own sense of well-being. Your means of expression can all too easily become blocked at the very same moment as your voice starts to change – dramatically breaking if you're a boy, more gently if you're a girl, but changing all the same. You start to hear yourself differently. People talk to you differently, often making you feel embarrassed and confused. It doesn't feel safe anymore!

In your desperation to escape being called a child, to belong to the bigger world, you forsake your childish ways and, with them, many of your childlike qualities. You become disconnected from the safety of being a child, being 'held' within the family. Energy which was once released so easily when younger may now get locked up inside. Teachers may start to accuse you of dumb insolence when you don't know what to say or how to say it. But you can't keep all the energy in! It breaks out, either in little bursts through your body or really big outbursts, shocking you just as much as the people around you – rows at home, fights at school! The words don't say what you really feel. All this energy is hurting, but it doesn't feel safe to say so!

As your friends start to play an ever bigger role in your life, you can find yourself in overdrive, trying to protect yourself from the cruel outbursts of words that young people throw at each other as they offload their excess energy. Whether the route you choose is extrovert or introvert, the strategy will be to continue to build an ever stronger wall of protection, either with words or silence. There's no doubt a wall of sorts is already in place, but now it is made thicker and higher! Maybe you won't even be aware you're doing it, but the feelings of frustration and anger will be there all the same, as you feel disconnected from what you desire almost more than anything else – to belong!

So Now You're a Grown Up

As you move towards the fullness of being an adult, your state of harmony is really put on the line. You may well go to college and meet a mix of people from all over the country or abroad. Again you experience what happened when you first went to school and it can feel just as shocking as before, with feelings ranging from excitement to dread. You may well have left home for the first time, with the added challenge of living with people you don't even know. The rhythms and tones of other people's families thrown together can create a very real feeling of confusion as you try yet again to belong. Alternatively, it could be the making of you, as you release yourself from the stifling rhythms and harmonies of home and school! You are both scared and excited at the same time. The only thing that limits you is you!

By now you are well and truly on *a* path, if not *the* path, to finding your place in the big wide world. Choices continue to be made. Role models continue to be copied. Maybe you join their orchestra, maybe you don't. But the pattern and rhythm established during your formative years will now come home to roost!

If you've been able to keep in touch with your own sense of harmony, you'll be on your way. You'll be able to adapt to the ever-changing energy around you, letting it in and out safely. The waves of energy that come at you don't swamp you or send you off course. You ride them with ease to help you on your journey. You know when to get off, you know when to let go, you know when to get back on. You know, too, when and how to reharmonize your own energy. You enjoy the route you've chosen towards your place in the world.

OK, maybe not! Is the journey still a bit confused? All too soon, as the pressure of the ever-expanding world grows on you to conform, to be adult, to be checking all the time what you say, you can start to feel a deep sense of loss. The fear of not finding somewhere to belong may put you in a permanent state of 'fight or flight'. You can start to suppress the joy of expressing who you really are and a little part of you may start to die. The frustrations and yearnings created by being made to conform yet wanting so much to belong have less and less opportunity to be released.

Year by year, the demand to be old before their time forces each new generation, at an ever earlier age, to take on the responsibilities of adulthood and to close down that part of themselves which can laugh and play and be silly. Their innocence gets lost, their spontaneity withers. Their sound gets blocked inside. Their life force becomes tamed and repressed. Who hasn't watched a friend passively sitting in front of the television and wished they'd go out and play and shout and sing? If they're not careful, they might have given up their most powerful means of bringing their bodies and minds back into harmony. And so might you!

This is the time in your life when, if you're out of touch with your natural state of harmony and well-being, you'll find yourself committing your life to a direction which not only doesn't help you to achieve your own state of harmony, but leads you further and further from finding where in this world you truly belong. Fear of getting it wrong, of failing to survive, will lead you towards believing everything everybody else says is where your happiness lies. You try to believe what they say is true, you want so much to belong.

This attitude can continue right through your life. 'It's better to be safe than sorry!' You could find yourself playing the piccolo, sitting with the violins, playing music you don't even like! Yet you still have a distant memory of wishing to be in a rock band, playing the drums! If you end up like this, your voice won't be your own. It will have instead a tone and sound which express the disharmony you feel in yourself and in your life.

SAFETY VALVES

If you're at all aware of the loss of emotional release that making sound can give you, maybe you've already found other 'outlets' to send back out the energy held within you.

Friends play a vital part in our release and exchange of emotional energy. Think for a moment about your friends. What's the mix of people around you? Haven't you sometimes said to yourself, 'I'd love to see Sarah, she's so up all the time' or 'I couldn't bear to see Michael, I don't feel strong enough to deal with him today'? We pick friends to shift our mood and state. What about when a friend calls you up, where do you come in their group? We all help each other towards our state of harmony. We all want to belong, to be part of the whole, even if we're not too sure where we're heading. It's natural!

There is, too, the ritual of releasing energy through making sound in harmony. Singing is a brilliant release used by many, whether it be in a choir or in the bath! The next football game or major pop concert you go to or see on television, really listen to the crowd. They're participants in a huge vocal release of emotional energy that needs and wants to come out. I remember watching the Live Aid concert in the 1980s and being overwhelmed by the sound, not just of the people on stage but the unbelievable power and energy given out by 100,000 people singing together with a passion.

These rituals of vocal release have been used for thousands of years. Going to the theatre, going to a film, going to a concert are also ritualized shared experiences. Each is a form of story-telling which takes us on emotional journeys, using sound or words or both. They provide an opportunity to let go of frustrations safely and express the joy of living. The days of the shamans are still alive and well! We've all come out of a cinema in tears, saying the film was wonderful. We've all felt elated by a piece of music which has shifted a feeling of apathy.

Most societies also choose alcohol as a 'legal unlocker'. It forms an excuse to the body to let go of energy in the form of sound. Why do so many people talk so loudly when they're drunk? Why do they feel safe to shout? Things they've wanted and needed to say at last start to come out.

If someone fails to find any emotional release by safely sharing their energy with others, however, they may well find themselves using alcohol only to numb the pain inside. Silently they sit and drink alone. No sound comes out.

Society itself has chosen to develop drugs in the form of tranquillizers and sleeping pills to suppress the need to release emotional energy. For many, their cry for help has officially been repressed. Nobody is prepared to listen to their pain.

The journey to becoming an adult isn't easy! To arrive at this point in your life, you'll have taken in and given out energy in the form of sound millions of times with hundreds of thousands of people, both in person and through the media. This energy moves us through the time and space of our lives, affecting and changing the state of our 'organized energy system'. We're all interconnected by this web of energy, which moves around our planet faster and faster in ever more complex forms. The harmony of the whole planet is affected by each of us and us by it.

Imagine standing on a trampoline with 30 other people. Someone on the other side sneezes, causing the person next to them to shift ever so slightly, causing the person behind them to shift, on and on until everyone on the trampoline is moving, trying to regain their balance. The whole trampoline will be in movement. It'll take ages for each person to regain their own equilibrium and just as long for everyone on the trampoline to become still at the same time.

Like the trampoline, if one person moves just a little, we're all affected. If one person speaks to another, we're all changed.

We all have the potential to find our natural state of harmony and equilibrium, the one we were born with. We all have the means to do as we did as a baby and express our needs and our dis-harmony by using our voices. But most us don't, out of fear!

CHAPTER FOUR

UNLOCKING THE FEAR

I was 21 and had been out of drama school six months. I'd just finished a production of a modern adaptation of Shakespeare's *Julius Caesar* for BBC Television, in which I'd played Octavius Caesar. I was asked to come back to the BBC and talk to some members of staff about what it was like to be an actor.

John Stride, who was then in his early forties, had played Mark Antony and was also asked to come and speak. He told some wonderful stories about playing Romeo in Shakespeare's *Romeo and Juliet* at the National Theatre in London, directed by Franco Zeffirelli.

When it came to my turn, I found myself saying what was uppermost in my mind. I'd just spent three years at drama school working to unlock my fear and find the freedom to again express my emotions freely. It had been painful and frightening at times, letting down my guard, starting to trust the people around me, feeling safe to show who I really was. When I'd finally faced my fear, I'd felt such a sense of elation and release. I told this room, full of highly professional television producers and directors, 50 members of the professional world I had recently joined, that what I'd found strange was, why was everyone so afraid?

They all froze. I'd said the unspeakable. I sensed them all physically pull back from me. I'd said the one thing that frightened them the most. The thing you just don't talk about. Fear! With my newfound confidence from drama school, I'd felt I wanted to tell them, 'It's all right, there's nothing to be afraid of, there's no need to hide.' Out of the mouth of a 21 year old, it didn't go down terribly well!

As I said, they all pulled back from me and went into varying degrees of 'fight or flight'. The power of the words had touched them, the energy had triggered their adrenalin and the first thing they did was to hold their breath. They tried to stop the feeling. The words had woken their memories of their own fears, which they immediately tried to block. Everyone, but everyone does it when they feel under threat and that's what they felt then.

When we hold our breath we can't feel anything. Try it, think of something that either makes you happy or sad or angry. Now hold your breath. Whatever emotions you're feeling won't be experienced until you breathe again!

What were they all frightened of? What were they trying to hide?

Another version of the phrase 'Everyone seems so afraid' is 'Hold still while I take your picture!' You freeze. The camera's cold eye is going to see something you don't want to show. You immediately put on your 'being photographed face'. You know the one? The one that hides who you really are? Imagine the lens coming ever closer, looking deep into your eyes. You hold your breath, your face freezes completely and then the photograph is taken. Everyone tells you, 'Just relax, be yourself.' You probably say that to other people too, but you never believe it yourself!

Next time you look through your photo album you'll see what I mean. If you look carefully at your adult photographs you'll see that despite all your efforts, the hidden part is there, in your eyes, in the way you're standing. Your mouth is trying to smile, but the eyes say something different. To others, you may look a bit tense, even when you're smiling. But you can see what is really going on, can't you? It 'leaks out', whatever you do.

But haven't you also got photos that were taken when you didn't know the camera was on you, photos which you really like, which show you just being you? They show the real joy inside you. Other photos, which may never have made it into the album, may show equally clearly your real sadness.

Asking people to say 'cheese' is just a way of getting them to breathe! For vast numbers of us, holding our breath is how we keep control of our feelings. Some of us barely breathe at all! The result is a voice which is higher and thinner than the one we'd use if we weren't so locked up. Our natural body note is deeper than you imagine. But you can't use it if you don't have any air!

What is it you're holding back? What are you stopping yourself from feeling? Haven't you ever watched a film when there was a moment which made you feel like crying? But you stopped yourself. You held on to the emotion you were feeling by holding back the tears. You held your breath. Why didn't you let yourself cry? What were you afraid of? Wasn't it appropriate? Did you feel silly? What were you remembering? What were the words and tones that triggered these emotions? What were you trying to keep the lid on? Is it a secret? Why won't you tell?

So What's your Secret?

People are silenced by their secrets! In all our lives there are things which we've never told anyone. We hold inside us many and various secrets. Secrets that we've kept totally hidden from the world, secrets we just don't want anyone to know.

Has anyone told you a secret recently? Said to you, 'Look, I don't want this to go any further, but...'? You listen and say, 'My lips are sealed.' You don't tell anyone. But you keep on finding yourself in conversations about the very subject of your secret. You have to 'bite your tongue' and hold your breath in case the secret slips out. You start to wonder, why is it so important not to tell? Everywhere you go you're about to be tripped up by someone and break your promise. It's a burden you wish you'd never been given, but you said you wouldn't tell! It's started to have a power over you. You wish you could find someone safe to tell. You end up telling your partner or a close friend and say to them, 'Now please, don't tell anyone, but...'

The secrets of our lives we hold inside are just as hard to keep hidden from the world. Every day you bite your tongue or hold your breath when you are taken back emotionally to something which hurt you or left you feeling guilty. Those secrets are shared with virtually no one and some are never told at all. People like to imagine they've managed to hide them away so successfully that they can forget about them. Yet you only have to look and listen to someone talking and you can tell whether something is being held on to, being hidden. Look and listen a little more carefully. The way a person moves and speaks is telling you almost exactly what it is. Some people are so contorted in the way they speak that it's clear they need to release this 'stored energy' which is hurting them so much.

Think of the people you've met who have great difficulty talking to anyone. Think of the people who never stop talking, but never say what they really mean. Think of those who can't bear silences and have to fill them. Think of those who never give you a straight answer. Think of those who never ask you a personal question in case you ask one in return, think of those who oh so fluently are 'economical with the truth'. Think of those who talk almost in a whisper in case anyone really hears them, think of those who look away all the time, trying not to hold your gaze. All of them are avoiding the truth of what they really feel, of who they really are. Yet most of the time you choose to say nothing, to pretend it's not happening. You help them to protect their secrets. You protect them from the person they don't want you to see and hear. You know they'd get very agitated if you stepped behind their mask and asked what's really going on. It would be too painful for them to expose that part of themselves they're trying so hard to keep hidden. So you join them in their strategies to keep you at bay. You go deaf and dumb for them. And quite possibly they're doing exactly the same for you!

Yet this is a state of false harmony. Ultimately it makes us all feel upset and angry and disconnected. We may spend years of our life with someone, never really knowing who they are, never giving each other the opportunity to express what we really feel. Always on guard, always ready to avoid, always feeling under attack, always fearful, we use many strategies to keep others from awakening those secret feelings. We'll silence their approaches using our status or power, if we have any. We'll attack them over something else to distract them from our most vulnerable areas. Each social group will create its rules and rituals of behaviour. The more inhibited they are, the more their etiquette is used to embarrass you into keeping 'off the grass' of their private secrets.

Language itself is used as a weapon to fend off a direct approach to emotions a person is trying to keep hidden. The clever phrase, the witty comment. But why do we do it? What secrets are we hiding? What lies behind this fortress of fear?

STORIES

All of us have secrets we've kept hidden from the world. Many believe they play no part in their adult lives. The truth is they're there, encoded in every word we utter. In all our lives there are some events which hurt us more than others, which have a dramatic effect on our need to be heard.

For virtually every person I've worked with, there was some key event, some time in their childhood, that blocked their voice. Someone told them to shut up. Not necessarily by using those words, but by deeply wounding them into silence.

All of the people whose stories I'm going to tell have very successful careers. Yet in the past every time they had to get up and talk, none of them could understand why they found it so difficult and why they got so nervous. All of them, I'm pleased to say, were able to rediscover their true voices.

These stories are not yours, but maybe there'll be some echoes of your own childhood within these people's lives.

Paul's Story

Paul was 45. He had a soft, rather tentative voice with an occasional stutter. He was always slightly wary, very charming, but his mood could change from friendliness to anger in a moment and suddenly his voice would be harsh and loud.

When he was 10, he always sat at the front of the class in school and was very much present in every aspect of classwork. If his teacher asked the class a question, he was always there with an answer. Paul wasn't backwards in coming forwards! He was cheeky but not rude. The teachers seemed to like him the way he was!

However, at the end of the school year, his teacher wrote on his school report that he was loud and precocious and disruptive to the class. She'd never said anything directly to him, so it came as a total shock. Paul just didn't understand what he'd done wrong.

From that time on, Paul retreated into himself. He felt so hurt. He never told anyone at school what the teacher had written and she never explained to him why she'd written it. He never wanted anyone to know how humiliated he'd felt and never wanted it to happen again. He retreated back into himself and become an outsider, an observer rather than a participant. Whenever he could, for the rest of his school career, he always found a way of sitting at the back of the class. His hand rarely went up to answer a question. He continued to feel he'd made some terrible mistake. Rarely would he get enthusiastic. If he did, he'd stop himself. He felt rejected and confused and lonely, but he never told anyone why.

With hindsight, Paul can look back and realize that perhaps he was too loud in class. Maybe the family he came from, who were always very vocal, didn't fit with the energy of the class he was in. The 'norm' wasn't the same as he'd been brought up to believe.

He realizes now that perhaps the teacher found him threatening or somehow he undermined her authority. Perhaps he needed more than his fair share of attention. The energy he gave out had swamped her. Perhaps he had triggered memories she couldn't deal with and she vented her anger on him instead – she shut him up rather than face the person she really needed to silence in her own life. But at the age of 10 Paul didn't understand. He just tried to cope with this crisis in the best way he knew how. The choice he made did get him through. No teacher ever accused him of being loud and disruptive again. He'd found a way to survive.

For now, just hold that boy in your mind while I tell you about Anna.

Anna's Story

Anna was 27 when I met her. Again, her voice was gentle, but it would fade away at the end of sentences. She also found it really hard to lift her eyes from the ground and look me in the face.

When she was nine years old Anna had a pet rabbit. She really loved her rabbit very much. When she came home one day from school to find it lying dead in the road outside her house, she was terribly upset. She knew her older sister had let it out of the cage, but the sister denied it.

When their mother came home, the older sister told her that Anna hadn't taken care of her rabbit properly and she'd killed it through neglect. Anna pleaded with her mother that this wasn't true, she loved her rabbit and wouldn't have done anything to harm it, but the mother believed the older sister. Anna was distraught beyond belief. No one in the family believed her.

It was never mentioned again, but Anna barely talked to anyone from that day on. The family didn't want to hear. She never told anyone her secret – that her parents thought she was a liar. She wanted to belong. The family strategy was not to talk about it ever again. So she stopped herself and it became a secret that she bottled up inside. But with it she locked up all the anger and hurt and rage at being treated so unkindly.

Perhaps the older sister didn't let the rabbit out, perhaps it was someone else. Finally, you could say, it doesn't really matter. But it mattered so much to the nine-year-old Anna. Her truth hadn't been heard, nobody had listened.

David's Story

David was 33, a very charming man, well liked by everyone. His voice was loud and strong and jokey in tone. He was the kind of man every woman wants to mother. He never liked to row or argue. If a situation arose when people around him were getting upset, he would try and joke everyone out of it. Yet what he was actually doing was saying, 'Please don't do this to me, I can't deal with it. You're frightening me.' People very rarely continued to row with him, but he continued to live in fear that they might!

When he was six, it had been suddenly decided that he was to go away to school. But his parents didn't explain why they were doing this to him in a way a child of six could understand. So he thought he had done something wrong. As their car disappeared down the drive, away from the school, he stood there sobbing. He had been left, deserted, by the people he loved and believed loved him too. The pain was unbearable. But he couldn't tell anyone how much he was hurting. The family strategy was to keep it all in. David developed his own strategy to keep the anger and pain from being heard: he became very charming and a bit of a joker. Nobody would ever find out how angry he was. He built up a defence mechanism to keep people out and to keep the feelings inside. It cost him the ability to really feel loved, to feel really safe.

I didn't run away screaming saying what a terrible person he was for having those feelings. His secret was out. His six-year-old boy was allowed to express what had been held inside for 27 years. He was finally allowed to be heard. The feelings he'd kept hidden inside were acceptable after all.

Each of us who feels the need to express ourselves more fully has a version of these stories – perhaps more than one story, perhaps many. We might not immediately be able to remember, but the energy surrounding them is still held inside, still there in our voices.

Only you can know your story. Only you can know how much it hurts. Only you can allow yourself to express that pain, however insignificant it may seem looking back. Finding someone you can trust to tell will release its power over your life. Finding someone to tell is the next stage of the story.

THE CHILD'S SECRETS

The secrets of our childhood have the biggest power over all of us, throughout our lives. Most of the time we try and pretend they didn't happen. We block out the memory or convince ourselves they're not our secrets anymore, they're in the past. But a part of us is still afraid that by telling someone, they'll stop loving or liking us anymore. We'll be cast out. We'll no longer belong. Others will realize how weak and pathetic we really are and dismiss us from their lives. But which part of us feels this?

However much we like to imagine we've left behind our past, the child we were is still there in everything we do and say. Try as you might to distance yourself with a veneer of sophistication, the child is still present. Someone can shout at you, using a tone of voice similar to your parents, and you'll freeze. Or you'll be driving and suddenly you see flashing lights in the rear view mirror and 'the voice of authority' tells you to pull over. You tell me you don't feel a child again!

The child knows all too well they need to express their pain, but they daren't. They know better than you that to get back to your natural state of harmony and equilibrium the energy must be released. But they also want to belong, to be included. So they're permanently on guard in case the secrets come out. They've remained in a permanent state of fight or flight, yet longing and hoping to find someone with whom they feel safe enough to release this overwhelming energy that's hurting them and you.

But they need to feel very safe indeed. These secrets may seem trivial to you now, but to the child in you, they matter very much.

This inner conflict is both exhausting and damaging to your very being. Until the secrets held inside are released, you'll never be truly heard. Until the child knows it's safe to tell, they will hold you back from feeling free to express yourself as fully as you might. This inner battle can be seen and heard every time we try to talk. The more public the talking, the greater the battle.

THE SOLDIER'S TALE

Some years ago a Japanese soldier was discovered in hiding on a small island in the Pacific. He'd lived for over 30 years, believing the Second World War was still happening. He'd been given no signs that it was over. There had been nothing out there to tell him it was safe to come out of hiding, safe to change the strategies he'd been using for all those years to survive. When I first read the story, I remember thinking how stupid. Surely he must have been able to work out that the war was over! But whatever signs he'd been given had only served to convince him even more that the war was still going on. To anyone who knew the war was over, those signs would have told a different story, but according to the information the soldier had had from 30 years before, nothing had changed. He had remained in his state of fight or flight for 30 years, until he was finally rescued. But all through that time he'd wanted so much for it to be over, to know it was safe to come out of his fear, back into the world.

If he were here now we could so easily laugh and scold him for being so stupid. Or we could have some compassion. After all, he'd been a very good soldier. He'd not been captured by the enemy. He'd survived for over 30 years. His strategy had worked! We could say to him, 'You've been a brilliant solder. You did the right thing based on what you knew then, but it's OK now, the war's over and we're going to look after you. We'll show you that it's safe to come out of hiding.'

We could say he was a child stuck in time. He hadn't grown up with the rest of the world in his knowledge of how things had changed.

The child in you, just like the soldier, has looked after you the best way they knew how, based on what they learnt about your world all those years ago. They remembered all your family fears for you, including all those of your parents and their parents before them; all the things you were told not to do when your parents shouted at you and made you jump; all the family secrets handed on from generation to generation. Your parents told the child in you never to tell anyone. Not in so many words, but your child knows your parents' very private hurts, having picked them all up while watching and listening and mimicking, as only a child can do. Each family orchestra always has a few tunes that belong to them alone!

But what about the secret that makes your child still cry out to be heard? Maybe they were made to feel inadequate. Maybe they were made to feel pathetic, stupid in some way. Maybe they still need to tell someone. Maybe they still need to let out all their rage. Maybe they need some real compassion and understanding for what they've been through. But what they also desperately need is not to be judged.

All of those children, in the stories I told you, felt they were inadequate to cope with what was done to them. Their world hadn't prepared them for what happened. Their family strategies, to survive and to belong, had let them down in a devastating way. In their desperation to find a way to still belong, to still be loved, they'd silenced their pain. They were determined never be made to feel like that again. But they'd all lived in fear that they might.

Each frightened child finds a way of never having to experience their pain again. They work out a strategy of survival to deal with the crisis in their lives, based on the world they were in at that time. But even as their world changes, every future crisis situation that feels as though it might take them back to how they felt when they were wounded will trigger the same strategy.

Over the years you may well try to block out any memories of your past pain. Yet whenever you're put under stress to communicate, it will all come flooding back – not necessarily the memory, but all the awful feelings!

The Frightened Child

You remember when I said the word 'afraid' to the BBC staff, they held their breath? Imagine the child in you is your emotions and they live in the place you lock up when you're under stress or afraid. The place which lets you feel. Imagine they live in the deepest recesses of your breathing. As I've already said, when you breathe, you feel. If you hold your breath, you can't feel a thing. If you breathe very shallowly, you can only feel a small amount. It's your breath that makes you feel alive. It gives you the energy in the form of oxygen you need for life. If you hold back on your breathing, you merely survive, you're not really living. But every time you try and express who you really are, by talking honestly and openly, the child in you panics that your secrets will be heard and locks up your breathing!

Also, every time you pretend everything's fine when it's not, your child is left to deal with that crisis on their own. You want to believe you've moved on, left those childish problems behind you, while the child is still trying to deal with them for you. The child needs you to listen to why they can't cope. But have you ever listened? Do you really care?

The Result

Let's imagine you're standing on a stage. Three thousand people are waiting for you to speak. The waves of energy in the auditorium are overwhelming. The child in you has ordered up a bulk supply of adrenalin, putting you into an extreme state of fight or flight – catastrophe mode! You start to perspire, to try and cool you down as the molecules in your whole body start to vibrate faster and faster. There's silence. You've already taken the three deep breaths they told you to take on the course you did, but nothing's coming out!

The butterflies in your tummy are going crazy – your child's shaking with drop-dead gut-wrenching fear, trying to cope with the situation you've put them into. They are living through their worst nightmare. Since the time you were hurt so badly they've used all their strategies to avoid this ever happening. But it's all coming back, those terrible feelings. They freeze up completely. Your breathing stops dead!

There's a voice, whispering in your ear, telling you how useless you are. You know the voice, the one who says things like, 'What's your problem, why can't you deal with it? You're so useless, can't you do anything right? Why do you always seize up and get so nervous? Pull yourself together, will you! If they see how nervous you are, you're going to blow it. Sure as eggs is eggs, you are going to blow it!' You're in the middle, wondering why this is happening to you, wishing someone would beam you up!

You try to put on a brave face. You start to talk. But your voice is shaking. The child is really upset, but you daren't listen! But the audience can hear your child in your voice! You try and relax, but your body starts to move like a child. You're out of control. Why isn't it coming out the way you planned? You try and control your breathing, try and cut off from what's going on down below and breathe higher up. The child is terrified and wants to blurt out all the pain, all the anger, all the rage. So you use as little air as possible. You try and look confident, but your face and body won't do what you want. Meanwhile the little voice in your ear is still telling you to give up and go home. You continue to wish it was all over! You go into close down, you switch everything off. You blank out. Where am I? Why am I here...?

That's a pretty bleak summary of events, but even if you're really good at conferences, the first time you go on prime time television live, you'll quite possibly know exactly what I'm talking about!

But most of your life is not spent at those extremes. In everyday life you don't feel under threat like that. Or do you? A new client you have to impress? Going to your boss to say they've screwed up, not you?! Someone, oh so nicely, trying to take your job away from you? Or calling someone in to tell them they've lost their job? Trying to explain to someone how to do something a better way when they don't want to listen? Your first meeting with someone you believe is going to transform your life? Having a row with your partner?

Of course you could be the kind of person who's not fazed at all when you get up and talk. Not by anyone or anything. You're not easily impressed. People are just people, nothing to get worked up about. Life's really a bit dull most of the time. One just has to get on with it.

I hope you're not, for your sake. But there's a lot of them out there. They've mastered the strategy of closing down, or so they believe. They switch off to such an extent that they tell themselves they don't feel anything. They're passive observers of life. When I meet people like that I listen and look through to their child. They're terrified, angry and sad. They know that no one will ever hear them. They've managed to convince themselves so totally that they must never ever show any real emotion whatsoever. No one must ever know how much they hurt. If you ask them, 'Are you happy?', they'll say, 'It depends what you mean by "happy".'

However well hidden you think your secrets are, the child inside is there, affecting your voice and your body. However good you think you are at hiding your very private self, others will know you're not being true to them, nor to yourself. The person we want and need to hear is *you*.

Your child requires you to be open and honest about the way you treat other people. Learning tricks to conceal your true self won't help you get back into harmony with yourself. The child knows this only too well. If you ignore their cries, all your efforts to find your place in the world where you'll be truly happy will be wasted. All the public success, recognition and money will never give you what you're searching for. The big home, the high status, the glossy lifestyle will mean absolutely nothing if nobody can hear who you really are.

THE VOICE IN YOUR EAR

You may be wondering who the voice at your shoulder was when you were on the platform delivering your speech? Well, it's another expression of your frightened child. They're also desperately wanting to behave like a grown up.

Some friends of mine have two children who are about four and seven. The seven year old, who has watched and listened to his parents, will tell the little four year old off, using exactly the same words and tones and rhythms as his parents did with him. He has become a miniature version of the adults. It's bizarre to watch, but I've been reassured by other parents that it's normal!

So, that little voice on your shoulder telling you how useless you are is another expression of your child attacking you and the child in your tummy for doing it all wrong and getting so upset! It's the child repeating all the telling offs you had from your parents or teachers when you were very young.

Next time you're with a friend who's genuinely laughing and giggling out loud, imagine them as their child at the age they were before they locked up, before they were terribly hurt. Each person has a different time in their childhood when they were first hurt and put in place their own 'personal survival strategy'. When they feel truly happy, they go back to a time before that event. They go back to the last time in their life they felt totally safe. David's would be, say, five, Anna's would be eight and Paul's would be nine.

There are other times when our child feels safe to come out and play. They're the times when we're having a perfect conversation.

CHAPTER FIVE

THE PERFECT CONVERSATION

Do you remember a wonderful conversation you had with a friend? A conversation when you felt you were really being heard, were really emotionally connected to another human being? Do you remember a conversation which gave both of you a deeper understanding of each other? You felt in tune, in harmony. For a fleeting time, you almost felt you knew what it was like to be one another.

If someone had been listening and watching, they'd have witnessed a musical duet of sound and energy, both instruments sharing the same melody and tune backwards and forwards with no effort at all. No one was leading. It was an expression of you both. It was shared. The thoughts were effortlessly expressed. Your voices were relaxed and open, there was no tension. You almost became one being, contained in a wonderful bubble of free-flowing energy. The rhythms and patterns of energy moved through and round you both in a magical harmony of sound and energy. You felt at one with the world and with yourself.

But why? Why was it so easy? Because the child inside both of you felt safe! Neither believed the other person was going to hurt them. The children came out to play. Both of you at some time had allowed the other to voice some, if not all, of their child's fears. Both of you had attended to the other's child by listening to what they were really trying to say and had responded to that part of them, rather than their mask. You did it in such a way that the other person felt it was totally safe to tell you things they'd possibly kept hidden for years. They told you their secrets! And what you probably did was to tell them yours. Not only to reassure them that they weren't alone in their fears, but also out of a respect for them for having felt you were worthy of their trust. There is a huge sense of release and relief knowing the other person didn't run away shouting, 'What a dreadful person you really are!'

With our true friends, we feel as though we could tell them almost anything and still remain safe in their friendship. We trust they won't judge us too harshly. We have, if we're lucky, an unconditional love for each other that makes us feel more in harmony with the world we live in, makes us feel good, makes us feel happy.

If you think about your close friends, you'll discover that you have incredibly similar fears hidden behind your masks. You'll also be aware that many of your childhood strategies to survive are similar too! If you look and listen carefully, you'll discover that your rhythms and tones will bear a remarkable resemblance to those of someone you felt safe with when you were both very young.

The elation both of your children feel, discovering they're not alone, that others have experienced similar pain and anger, will bond you together. Even when you first met, there may have been a sympathetic resonance. You could hear their child calling and you felt comfortable with their energy. You have become 'family' to each other. And, just like family, if you're out together in the world, you'll cover for each other when new people are introduced, protecting each other's child from being hurt. Well, as I've said before, ideally!

So What's Going On?

Whether you are the speaker or the listener in any conversation, you engage in an exchange of images, thoughts and emotions. You don't think in carefully tailored sentences. You don't **speak** in sentences either! When talking with a close friend, you'll say, thought by thought, what's in your mind. They'll echo your every word and tone under their breath. You'll both breathe and experience what you've just said at the same moment. You'll check out whether they've understood by watching their faces and bodies. You'll also check whether you yourself understood what you've just said! Your friend will nod involuntarily if they're still with you! And so will you, as if to say, 'I know you know.' You both experience what you've said at the same moment. Magically there in your mind will be the next thought ready to be spoken. Like building blocks, one thought is put on top of the next.

When you've completed the cycle of thoughts, you'll review them as a whole. In that moment, as you both breathe, you'll decide between you who's going to carry on the speaking. A true conversation will be an expression of you both. Even when one person is doing all the talking, the other person is always part of the process. You'll always be trying to stay in step with each other – sitting or standing the same way, moving and breathing together, echoing the words under the breath to gain an even deeper understanding what it feels like to be the other person. If one person shifts position, the other will follow. If one starts speaking more quickly, when the other takes over they'll keep up the pace. Neither of you will own the conversation. It belongs to you both.

If someone heard your conversation through a wall, it would be hard for them to tell from the sounds and the rhythms who was speaking and when one person finished and the other began. You'd be so in harmony, you'd sound as though you were one voice. Even if you were having an argument!

This is an example of what goes on in your special relationships, the ones you cherish and nurture. Hurting them would be to hurt yourself.

Most people have grades of friendship. The closer your friends are, the more they'll know about you. Those who you feel less safe with will know less, until you get to your passing acquaintances, who know virtually nothing about you, except your outer mask. Few of us have more than a handful of people with whom we feel safe enough to be totally ourselves. This doesn't necessarily mean that when we're with them we are in total harmony with ourselves, but they can help us to get nearer to that feeling.

Those wonderful conversations we have with our friends don't, however, tackle the problem of releasing the child from the pain of the past. They're merely islands of safety in a hostile world! You'll feel comfortable knowing you are not alone with your fears, that someone else feels similar to you. But the fears can still remain hidden from the rest of the world. You can still spend every single day of your life meeting and talking to people with whom you're afraid to be genuinely open. What a terrible waste! So why is it you don't feel like you do with your best friends every time you talk to someone?

First Meetings – the Reality!

Let's start with when you meet someone for the first time. Every new person is a new possibility. Maybe they'll become your best friend, your lover or your business partner. Maybe they'll hurt you in some way. Maybe they'll beat you up. Maybe they'll cheat you in business. Maybe they'll get close to you and then reject you. Maybe they'll be the person you've been waiting to meet all your life, the person who'll lead you on to your natural place within the world. Maybe you'll wish you'd never met!

Even before the other person speaks, a wave of energy comes from them into your body, making you feel both frightened and excited. Their very presence has an immediate effect on you. You try to feel exactly where they're 'coming from'. But who's doing the feeling? Your frightened child? Is your guard up? How high is it?

The more afraid you are, the less you'll sense! If your child is coming from a place of extreme fear, you definitely won't be listening, looking and feeling from a place of harmony! You'll be judging the new person based on the tiny amount of information which has got past your barriers. What's more, your child, as we now know, will be working with an understanding of the world which is out of date! And, guess what, the other person will probably be doing exactly the same with you! And you haven't even said hello yet!

If both of you are very guarded, each will be wary of what the other is hiding. But what is it?! In this moment of fear, you may both freeze, while trying to gauge each other. Who's going to come out of hiding first? Who's going to make the first move, even if it's only by the tiniest amount? Who's going to disclose a part of themselves to let the other person feel safer? What part will be opened up to scrutiny and by whom? 'Why do they want to talk to me? What do they want from me? Who are they really? Is it safe to tell them who I really am? Will it help me survive?' The more in harmony you are with yourself, the more prepared you'll be to make it easier for the other person. If you so choose!

However, usually you'll be given a bit of help! Someone you already know may introduce you and you can use them to check whether it's safe to open up. Your friend may have already told you a bit about the new person beforehand, reassuring you they're OK. Or, hawklike, you may be able to listen and watch to find out how the new person behaves with your friend. You check that against how you feel about your friend and then make a judgement as to how much you're prepared to lower your guard. So, if you already like your friend and they're feeling really comfortable with this other person, you might jump right in there and risk it! Well, you might! Of course, remember the other person will be doing exactly the same with you!

What I'm describing can feel like war and for so many people that's just what it is! For them, meeting people is not about love and affection and being in harmony, it's about basic survival! Wouldn't it be wonderful if they felt safe enough to talk to the real person every time they met someone, instead of remaining in emotional turmoil, living an imitation, an illusion of real life based on their fears?

So, how do you talk to someone whose barriers cut them off from really hearing what you're saying?

TAKING DOWN THE BARRIERS

About eight years ago, when I was 35, I was in hospital. There was a nurse on the ward who never spoke to me – she shouted at me, even when she was only at arm's length from my ear. Her 'professional voice' was talking to me as if I were a stupid three year old. This was the voice she used with all her patients, young and old. I wonder how the three year olds in the next ward reacted?

There are many people in this world who talk to children and adults just like that all the time! But children are usually much brighter than we give them credit for. Also, most of them aren't deaf! Neither are they as frightened as adults about talking to people – not yet!

Watching and listening to children before they've been 'locked up' emotionally is a revelation as to how you can be with another human being. If you can find again the openness and harmony of a child, you'll have the beginnings of how to reach the child in every adult you meet and talk to.

Talking with a well-adjusted young child can either be a wonderful or terrifying experience. Many people don't know what to say to them and can't bear the way the child looks and speaks straight through their mask to their own child. The little person talking to them hasn't yet felt the need to learn the strategies to hide their true selves. They're still in harmony! A person who's locked their child away will find it almost impossible to find a level that the child will be able to relate to. The child will look at them quizzically, wondering what's going on. They know what's being presented to them is sus-pect, that it's not real. But they won't know how to play the adult game of saying, 'I'll pretend what you're presenting to me is you, if you pretend what I'm presenting to you is me.' They know who they are! They're waiting for the adult to get real and talk child to child, person to person!

This is when some adults attack children for being too direct. They'll use their most aggressive strategies to keep this little person away from their own child. The rage and fear of their own child, who isn't able to be heard, turns into aggression and is dumped on the child standing in front of them. In fact this can be the very moment when the child in front of them becomes locked up emotionally.

If you can really talk to a child, though, you can talk to anyone. They're closer to what it's really like to be in harmony than you are. By listening and watching, they'll teach you what talking from a place of harmony is really all about. They can be your 'role model' to unlock the child inside you who wants to be allowed to come out and play.

TALKING TO A FRIGHTENED CHILD

Let's imagine a three-year-old child came running up to you who'd been frightened by something. Ideally, you'd attend to their fears, ask them what the matter was in a tone of voice which was neither threatening nor condescending. You'd be listening and watching, helping them to know you're really with them, that they're really safe. You would give them your time. You would attend to them. You'd put your own fears on the back burner. Your voice would naturally adjust to theirs. This doesn't mean you'd squeak, but you'd use a tone which was in harmony with theirs, gently calming them down or alternatively bringing their energy back up until they were again in harmony with themselves. You'd stay with them until they felt safe.

This is the way to reach every frightened child you meet. Whether they're little or large, they all need to be heard. What you don't do is shout at them, saying, 'What are you getting so upset about? Pull yourself together, you stupid child!' What you're then doing is demanding the child to lock their feelings back inside, because they're making your own child feel upset! The sound of a child crying will resonate with your own cries, bringing feelings back up to the surface which maybe you've been trying to keep buried. But if you can comfort the frightened child in front of you, maybe you can do the same for the child in you.

TALKING TO YOUR CHILD

You now know you're not alone in having this very scared part of you. Virtually every person you meet has got one too! And until their child feels safe, you'll never be able to really talk to them. But until you've learnt to talk to your own child, you'll never be able to talk to anyone else's. Until you've really listened to your own child's pain and then to what makes them happy, you'll never be able to reach that part in other people. So they'll never be truly listening to what you say.

How do you begin to talk to your child? You talk just as you would if you met any child who's very upset: you reassure them that you'll hang in there and always be there for them to help them through any difficulties they may have, day or night, respecting what they've done for you in the past to help you survive.

Your child isn't just the one who gets frightened or gets in a rage. Your child is the one who gets ecstatic. Your child is the one who has amazing dreams. Your child is the one with a wild and vivid imagination. Your child is the one who is stunningly creative. Your child is the one with passion and energy and life. Your child is magical. Your child is your route back to you. Your child knows better than you do what it feels like to be in harmony. Your child is the one who needs to be heard!

It may sound strange, but if I get really tense when I'm about to meet someone, my child is actually out of my body and walking along beside me. I'm holding his hand as we walk along together. I've made it my job to help him feel safe. I attend to him. I listen to him, just as if I were his manager or agent or ideal father. If he starts to tense up, I listen to him and talk him through what's bothering him. Once he feels safe, he then helps me back to my own state of natural harmony. He takes me back to that part of me who can be just as content and happy as he is. We've agreed to work as a team. He'll do what he's really good at, which is to talk to others' children. If it gets really tricky, he knows I'll bail him out with my adult expertise, but only if it's needed. He says 'Hi' to someone's child while I say 'Hi' to their adult!

If you can find a way of working with your child, instead of ignoring them, you can achieve together your place in the world where you'll both be happy to be happy. And what's more, you'll be able to talk to anyone without fear ever again!

OTHER PEOPLE'S CHILDREN

If you are to really talk to someone, their child needs to feel safe enough to come out and play. If they don't, they won't and they'll use all their strategies to keep you at bay. But if you're in touch with your own child, you can show theirs that it's safe. Like a parent playing with a child, it won't matter who's the parent and who's the child. You'll be able to help each other to feel again what it is to be in harmony; you'll be able to help each other to move towards your rightful place in this world.

There are people you'll have met who make you feel safe, not because they are 'confident', but because they've nothing to hide. Their child is present in everything they say and do. Their child isn't frightened of being heard; they know they're safe. Nobody can hurt them. Not even you! So when you met you felt it was safe to be honest and open and truthful and really talk to them. In return they heard your child and in less than a moment you talked from a different place and it felt wonderful. It really is possible to make the leap!

I'd like you to take a few moments and think of the speakers you most admire. They may be friends or colleagues or public figures, perhaps a newsreader or a presenter. Think about what it is you like about them. Is it their dour personality? Is it the fact that they're dull and lifeless? No, it's because you really feel they're talking to you! Even with those who still have a bit of a mask in place, you can see and hear their child, who's not too frightened, telling you how they feel. It may be just a twinkle in their eye, expressing their delight in talking to you. But the child is there, having a pretty good time, feeling safe and secure to come out and be seen and heard for who they really are – a wonderful person who's living a very real life!

You may or may not like her, but Oprah Winfrey, who's won a considerable number of Emmy awards for her work and who just happens to have been an actress before she did her talk shows, is a grown up child. I'm not talking about child*ish*, I'm talking about child*like*. Her child listens, asks the questions and talks to you. She is appealing, she has charisma, she is enchanting to millions of people! She can also be very serious and emotionally available. She has very little to hide. Her child may still be a bit frightened sometimes, but she still comes out to play. She's not in hiding!

I mention Oprah because her show is seen all over the world. I'm not going to suggest you should be like her. Your child will be totally different. But she is someone who has got nearer than most to being happy with her child in a very pressurized and public environment.

There is for me someone who I believe is the most wonderful example of a child coming out to play. I remember going to hear the Dalai Lama, the leader of Tibetan Buddhism throughout the world, when he spoke in London a couple of years ago. As he came onto the stage he was greeted by enormous applause. He suddenly noticed someone he knew in the audience and came to the front of the stage to say a few words to them. He was laughing and giggling as he went back to the microphone and told us that he'd not seen the person for over 10 years and how thrilled he was to meet them again. He included us in his pleasure. Then he spoke for more than an hour without notes, moving his audience from laughter to tears and back again with what he was saying. He had no fear, we couldn't hurt him, he was hiding nothing. There were no barriers between us, all 10,000 of us.

Someone who is totally open cannot be hurt. There is nothing to attack. Remember, what causes people to go on the defensive or to become aggressive, to go into a state of fight or flight when you talk to them, is their fear of exposing their secrets.

The Dalai Lama laughs like a child and speaks with the wisdom of centuries. He's not only wise with childlike qualities, he is indeed a wise child. There are many others whom I'm sure you know and like. Watch and listen to their child, which will be there, talking and listening to the child in you.

Alternatively, you will know when someone isn't being real. I'm not going to give any examples! But now you know what's going on, you'll appreciate when someone is trying to be something they're not, trying to hide a very terrified child. However much they try to conceal it within the sounds and words they use, their voice will be telling their story, echoing their past pain. As you get better at listening and watching you'll almost be able to tell what the child's trying to say from behind the carefully placed mask.

Andrew's Story

Andrew was 31 and wanted to be an actor. He was doing a speech I'd asked him to learn. It was really dreadful! He had a tough London accent which was so mannered and forced. Mr Macho! He hit all the wrong words, making nonsense of what he was saying. I despaired and asked him if he knew any other accents he could use for the speech. He told me he could 'sort of' do one from southwest England.

As he started to speak, the words that came out of his mouth suddenly had real meaning. He was talking to me! As he found the accent more precisely, he started to cry as the words flowed out of him with a wonderful ease and fluency. He said the speech beautifully.

When he'd finished, he told me his story. He'd been brought to London by his mother when his parents divorced and had gone to a school in a tough area. All the children had made him feel stupid because he had a funny accent, so he'd tried to copy the way they spoke as quickly as he could, just to survive. But it wasn't a natural process of change. It was forced and fake.

By going back to the accent he used to have, he was able to be himself and speak from the heart the speech he'd been given to say. The strategy he'd used 20 years before, to survive, to belong, had stopped him expressing the sadness of his parents' divorce. But he'd also cut himself off from all the happiness he'd felt as a young child.

When you've completed our work together, talking with someone, talking to a small group of people or talking to millions, whatever, your child will be there with you, having a great time, instead of being terrified. You'll share with them their happiness that they've finally been heard. You'll both know you are finally on your rightful path to being truly alive and truly happy.

But first we're going to look in more detail at how you and your child can help each other to say what you really feel in the two most important areas of relationships in both your lives. By understanding what is going on you'll both be able to help each other to fulfil your potential and speak to anyone.

ADULTS YOU MEET ALONG THE WAY

Two of the most crucial areas in our lives, where the way we talk to people really matters, are in our very private life and in the place where we work. Both can bring us real fulfilment, both can bring us very real pain. All too easily we can make a real mess of it if we don't talk child to child!

YOUR LOVER

Remember your first date? Sweaty palms, heart racing. Energy going all over the place as you hung in there. Not knowing what to say, what to talk about. Laughing and smiling all at the same time. Playing the fool, being the child. Wanting the other person to like you. Afraid of being rejected. Being frightened and excited all at the same time. Frightened that you'd say too much. Using all your strategies to survive, but wanting to throw them all away and tell the other person everything. Wanting to tell them all the things that mattered to you, but you just didn't dare! Oh the pain of it, oh the joy!

Maybe yours was different, but I feel sure there were some elements which were exactly the same as everyone else's!

That first date may by now be far behind you, but the very thought of it will fill you with embarrassment as well as fond memories of the innocent anticipation of what was to come. If you're lucky you'll have experienced in your life a closeness with someone where you could be entirely yourself. The barriers were totally down and they still loved you! When a relationship between two people is really working well, they both feel safe to be whatever age they want at any given moment. Their children feel safe to come out and play and voice their fears freely without having to pretend they're feeling something different. At last each person's child can be heard.

Using baby talk is all part of how couples make contact with each other's child. Sometimes, though, when they can't find the bridge between the child and adult worlds, it can become a form of play-acting because they're still afraid to just talk to each other as equals.

But for many, the relationship with their lover is the only one in their life where they're prepared to allow another person to hear and see their child. Not even their best friends get that close! It can be the only time they allow themselves to experience an emotional intimacy with another human being. I don't just mean sexual, but emotional. Most of the barriers are down and the exchange of secrets bonds the two people together. They want to believe they've found their soul-mate who understands their pains and forgives them all their rage. They long to feel at last there is someone with whom they can truly feel safe from the harshness of the world outside. They want to feel that at last they're loved unconditionally.

Most people choose a partner who speaks the same 'language' as their own family. They'll also pick someone with many of the same fears. It makes their child feel comfortable, if not happy, to know that the other person's child has experienced life in a similar way to themselves. If both their families were open and easy, it has the chance of being a good and healthy match and each child will feel safe. If they're not from healthy families, the relationship may well be used to work out past fights and feuds all over again.

The sexual urge can hurtle us towards an intimacy which is fraught with danger for the frightened child. Every fear, every desire and every need is magnified by the speed of events. Our sexual energy and excitement can overpower our senses and so easily be confused with our fears. Both emotions will trigger adrenalin, both feelings have more in common than we sometimes imagine.

Our lover can be the person who becomes our best friend and just as easily the person who can hurt us the most. The mask we use with them can end up being bigger and more difficult to remove than the one we use with anyone else, as we pretend to be something we're not, out of the fear of losing them. Many couples find themselves living a lie about who they really are, so frightened are they of showing their true feelings. We all know people who tell us things they'd never tell their partner under the pretext 'it would hurt them to know'. In fact they are the one who is frightened of their partner finding out, of their partner knowing who they really are.

All too easily this intimate relationship can be based on keeping our fears and secrets hidden, from each other, as well as the outside world. The complex web of energy becomes part of our conspiracy of untruths. We feel lonely in our supposedly most intimate and open relationship. The hope of having found an ally behind our mask but still keeping the rest of it in place with everyone else leaves us even more isolated from our real selves than before! The energy remains hidden in a closed world. There is no release. The expectations that our partner will heal all our pain and magically take away all our fears can be too much for the other person to cope with. So even in this presumed intimacy the relationship may not be based on true love and affection but on a lie. We're petrified our partner will find out who we really are and angry that they don't!

Some couples stay in this madness for the whole of their lives. No one else can understand why they stay together. They're playing out an ancient story of love and pain and rejection, avoiding an honest intimacy, repeating it over and over again, still waiting to be really heard, but not brave enough to say what really hurts. Each child is so angry that the other person isn't really hearing them, isn't solving their fear, that they wound one another out of rage. Until one day, maybe, one of them escapes!

If each person has remained fearful of the outside world, the ending only adds to their sense of anguish – not just because they've lost someone they believed they loved, but because they feel betrayed at having lived under such emotional scrutiny, only to find all the pain and fear they endured didn't help them to be heard. They believe they'd shown someone who they really were and then lost them, yet what they'd most probably done was to pretend to be someone they weren't and been found out!

If this happens, it takes the child a very long time to be convinced it's safe to come out of hiding again! The barriers, understandably, go back up and a promise is made by the child never to trust anyone with their most private self ever again.

But most people move on, tentatively lowering the walls when they can, praying they won't be so hurt again, longing to feel it's safe to be themselves. The search goes on to find someone who loves and accepts them for who they really are. The only problem is, will they really tell them?

If your intimate relationships are based on the expectation of the other person magically healing all of your pain, it's not going to work. Your child needs to start to feel safe with you first, needs to feel you understand what's hurting them, before they'll feel safe enough to fully commit to building a relationship of such intensity and intimacy with another human being. Being scared to show who you really are to someone who will come to know you better than anyone else isn't the best recipe for future personal happiness. But if you and your child can begin the process of talking to each other without evasion, you'll begin to be able to do the same with the other person's child. Only then will you and your partner start to hear what each other is really saying and really asking. Only then will you be able to find together where your happiness truly lies. Only your child can open the door on a different way of being, but they'll need your help to climb up and reach the lock!

THE WORKPLACE

Every aspect of your ability to communicate with people is present in the workplace. When we talked about your childhood we talked about family, how the family you were born into was your first world. School was your second and your work is your third. We relate to every stage of our lives based on our family strategies. Each of the worlds we move into is structured like a family, good or bad. The community you live in is the other family which you are a part of and which affects your well-being. It will be made up of people you know well and those you have passing contact with every day of your life. How you move through your life will depend very much on how well you are able to be yourself, how available you've made your child to talk to the people you meet along the way.

The added dimension for most people in the workplace is a double dose of FEAR in capital letters, especially in this day and age where no one feels safe in their job. SURVIVAL is also rather high up on most people's agendas! Yet most organizations will present themselves as a safe place that cares about the people they employ. How true is this? Many people give their lives to a company without realizing the company hasn't actually given itself to them. Big corporations are 'organized energy systems' living in fear, in a permanent state of 'fight or flight'. If for a moment you think of a company as a very frightened child you'll begin to understand what I mean. Their strategies are all based on FEAR and SURVIVAL. Remember how the company always comes first!

Most people see the workplace as the most dangerous place in the world for them to open up. The most dangerous place to be themselves. The most dangerous place to allow their child to be heard. Every strategy in the book is used to hide the child from being exposed, just in case someone uses it against them. Yet it can be where most of your waking life is spent. It's where you'll probably be talking to different people all day long. It can also be the place where you live out the most important part of your life. But do you live or do you just survive?

Let's just run through a few of the kinds of people you are likely to meet and the strategies they use to survive in this rather hostile environment. See whether there's anyone you know. Remember, it's their child who's doing the talking.

Personal Strategy Types

The Status Seekers

Whenever their child feels under threat these people will use their status to keep you back from reaching their angry child. The more insecure they are, the more important they will try to be. They may be charming or abrasive, but the line you must not cross will be taken with them everywhere they go. Imagine them as seven years old and you'll know what I mean. Their authority isn't a natural authority born out of a well-balanced level of self-esteem. Their voices will have a tone which is condescending, as if they were talking to a stupid child. It will be the tone of voice that was used by someone on them.

Certain of my clients have status that others would die for, but because they're comfortable with themselves as people, they never feel the need to flaunt it. Those who crave it themselves are always staggered at how 'normal' these people are, how their status doesn't seem to have affected them in the slightest. Maybe they got there by not using status games in the first place!

The Teasers

They too speak to you as if you were a stupid child – their stupid child! They will crack a joke at everyone else's expense, but not their own. If you do it to them, they'll sulk. Though they like you to believe there's a smile in their voice, there will always be a hard edge from their past cutting through to wound. That edge is the person who wounded them as a child – a teacher, a parent, someone who cut them to the quick. They want you to *feel* their pain, but they'll never tell you why.

The Super Cools

We've all seen and spoken to those people who make you do all the work. They may or may not have status, but they're terrified of losing face or making a mistake or, dare I say it, letting you see or hear who they really are. They are invariably copying a stereotype they've seen in the media. Especially if they are in the media! Their voices are carefully modulated and controlled all the time and their breathing is restricted. They're desperately trying not to feel anything, desperately trying to give nothing away. Yet if you watch their eyes, they'll be checking nervously all the time, listening in on every other conversation to be sure there's no chance of someone catching them off guard. Yes, super cools are terrified too!

The Over-Energized Needers

With these people, so needy is their child to be heard, to feel safe and loved and protected, they'll do almost anything to stop you shouting at them, telling them off or being unkind. Over-keen to please, they're seemingly listening to your every word but desperately wanting you to listen to them. Their need will pour off them. Yet it's just as much a strategy to survive. They're just as angry as the status seekers but they just aren't on a rung of the 'ladder' which lets them do a power trip. If they have status over someone they invariably use it with a vengeance. Not wanting to sound at all threatening, they'll have a higher voice than their natural body tone, but it changes to a harsh screech when they think they have status.

The Cultivated Charmers

This is a more strategic form of the above. You nearly believe the child has come out to play, but the performance is so polished and plastic you know no child can be that smooth. The charmers 'present' themselves to everyone, high or low, but behind their mask lies a very sad and lonely child that no one is ever allowed to see. In fact they've created a perfect shield that they find almost impossible to penetrate themselves! Their warm tone will wrap you in honey, but there will be the occasional sharp tone in their voice, just like a bee sting!

The Theatricals

I hasten to say not all actors use this voice, but some do. It is intended to draw your interest, to gain your attention, to let the person be heard. The theatricals are the most transparent of those who need to be heard. Their voice is usually loud, sweeping and flowing beautifully, all to hold your attention, but all too easily it can sound false. They really do need to be loved. No one loved them just for themselves. They always feel they have to earn it.

The Hard to Get

These people will make it so hard for you to reach them. They are lost in their sadness, not believing anyone will ever climb over their barriers and want to reach them. Every time you try to get close they'll move back out of reach until you despair and give up. They'll have proved themselves right again, you didn't want to reach them enough! Their voices will have bursts of energy, but will fade off in mid-sentence.

The Wary Ones

They want to be reached, but are terrified of letting you in. They're similar to the hard to get, except they will let you in. But it will all have to be very secret and you must not tell anyone what they tell you, ever! Their voices will be quiet and secretive and they'll be listening and watching everything you say and do – just in case!

The Vocal Bully

These people are angry because no one listened to their pain. They're angry at the world for ignoring their child's need. They're angry at everyone and everything. Nothing's ever right. They make a lot of noise, but it's never about what's really hurting them. They use their voice to hurt and wound. So aggressive is their energy no one feels safe to get close and the anger just grows and grows.

The Resenters

These are the ones who wish no one well. If someone else is happy, they'll do them down usually very quietly. If someone's done something of note, they will exclaim, 'Oh, they were just in the right place at the right time.' They resent people doing all the things they wish they could do but daren't. They say they wouldn't want to be like the people they attack, but sadly they do! They're just as angry as the loud ones, but they don't make as much noise. Their voices are harsh and quiet, but deadly!

The Adaptors

Most of us have been caught out with this one at some time in our lives. Adaptors shift from one mode to another. Different people are presented with different personalities as they adjust very adeptly from one persona to another. They all too easily lose touch with who they really are. The child's message is usually simply, 'Love me whoever I am.' They'll do anything to get you to love them, so desperate is their need. Such people are fairly difficult to pin down, because they're the most able to adapt to change. Their main problem is they have so many masks! Their voice will change from person to person, mimicking the voice of the person they're with. Their biggest nightmare is all their friends being in the same room at the same time! Rarely will you be invited to a party with all of them present!

The Carers

These have a very modulated voice which has been trained to make you feel at ease. But it's just that bit too careful. A lid has been put on their own emotions. Very often they wish someone would listen to them as carefully as they are forcing themselves to listen to you.

Quick, Before You Go

These are people who speak very quickly with quite a high voice, never pausing for breath. They are frightened they won't be able to finish what they're saying before you run away. Someone did that to them when they were very young and they so desperately want to finish what they're saying both to you and to them.

The Chatterbox
These sound very similar to the above, but they don't want themselves to hear what they really feel, let alone you! By talking all the time about anything and everything, they try to drown out their child's pain. They're terrified to stop in case they start to tell you what they're really feeling. They don't mind who they're talking to, because what they're saying doesn't really matter, even to them. They might not even be aware it's you they're talking to!

The Lazy Articulators
These are people who have given up on believing anybody really wants to hear what they have to say. Very often they speak very quietly, as well as not speaking clearly, so you have to ask them to repeat themselves. It becomes so awful and all because they didn't think you'd want to hear them in the first place.

The Turn of Phrasers
These use words as a means of protection. They will always turn what you say into something else. They will never answer your questions simply. It's as if by using complicated language they will never have to be confronted with who they really are. They're also known as jargoneers. Very sharp, very quick and very lonely. They have modulated and clear articulation, slightly clipped, with no gaps to let you hear who they really are. Politicians are notoriously good at this strategy!

The Switched Off and Safe
Here, nothing penetrates, nothing comes out. These people try not to feel anything. They're not moved by anything. These are the ones who quietly get very ill as their energy grows stagnant. Nobody can hurt them. Nobody reaches them, they're unheard and unseen. These are the hardest to reach or talk to, grey people who are so terrified of

their pain and anger getting out they place such a tight lid on their emotions that they're hardly alive. They hide away by finding somewhere to live their lives without making waves of any kind. They either explode one day and release this burden of energy they hold inside or they quietly disappear with nobody ever knowing they were there. Such people will have tried to 'de-voice' themselves. Their voice will come from their very tight throats as they try to contain and bury their emotions.

The Cute Child

This is where an adult has got stuck in replaying their childhood over and over again by using a childish voice. It can sound very appealing indeed. It's meant to! It was a strategy voice they created to get what they wanted when they were very young. We all use it from time to time to get us out of trouble, but they use it all the time! They are now terrified of being judged as an adult. Yet underneath they're full of rage at the person who wouldn't let them grow up and only showed them any love if they used this cutesie voice.

These are just a few examples of people's strategies. They help them survive, but I'm afraid they don't help them to live as fully as they could! All of them are re-affirming their fears every time they speak. The tones and rhythms they use affect their bodies and minds too, trapping them in their own strategies, making it harder and harder for their child to be heard.

If you bring to mind anyone you know who fits one or other or a combination of these states and think about their child, you'll start to understand what's really going on when you talk with them. Unlike talking to a well-adjusted child, these people's children will be shaking with fear and rage behind their masks. Yet none of them can imagine how wafer thin their mask is!

By listening and watching what their child is trying to communicate and by responding more and more to that part of them, you'll begin to gain their trust. I wouldn't advise shouting at them, 'Come out, come out, wherever you are!' It doesn't tend to work! And if you continue to keep your own mask in place, they too will carry on as before. But if you and your child are speaking from the same place of harmony, their child will hear you and start to feel safe. The person they really are will begin the process of coming back out to play.

With all of these different types of childhood strategies in mind, I'm going to show you a practical example of how you can begin to talk to someone's child. We're going to look at a very simple and basic conversation which takes place on the phone. Telephones are the medium some people love and some people hate. You only have the voice, nothing else. For those who want to be someone else they feel safer. For those who need to see the visual clues as to whether it's safe to talk, they're a nightmare. Virtually everyone has a telephone voice which is a heightened form of what they do if they meet someone face to face. But who they really are can still be heard. You only have to listen.

I'm not going to take you through all the variations which you have to encounter every day, but let's look at a conversation when two people speak to each other for the very first time on the phone. We normally start a conversation with a new person with our barriers in place. Only when we feel really safe will we start to let them down.

Let's look at the opening of the call.

David: Hello, is that Helen Roxborough?
Helen: Yes, it is.
David: Hi, I'm David Montgomery.
Helen: Hi.
David: Michael Davies said it would be OK if I called.
Helen: Oh, right.
David: He said you might be able to help me with an article
        I'm writing.
Helen: Oh, what on?

How did that sound to you? The way you read those few lines to your-self says quite a bit about where you're coming from at the moment! You'll have voiced the words in your head by silently mouthing them with variations of your own voice. You'll have said them to yourself and decided which one was nearest to you and given the other voice to someone who has affected you recently, for good or for bad. Though they'll both be variations of your own voice. It's your ver-sion! It's how you'd have reacted if those words had been said to you.

Now let's add a layer of simple fear – not masked, but obvious in the voice. Just imagine Helen's child is very distrustful of anyone she doesn't know. David is relaxed and open. Run the words again and see how different it sounds in your head.

Now imagine Helen is open and relaxed, but David's child assumes no one really wants to help him, let alone talk to him.

Now run them both being very frightened. The words will be the same, but the tone of each of their voices will change.

You can now try using any or all of the 'Personal Strategy Types' I've already described and imagine how they would sound to you.

Now, remembering how we decided to talk to a frightened child from the last chapter, let's imagine Helen is very open and easy, but she's aware of David's frightened child and wants to make it eas-ier for him to talk to her.

David: Hello, is that Helen Roxborough?
Helen: Yes, it is.
David: Hi, I'm David Montgomery.
Helen: Hi.

David: Michael Davies said it would be OK if I called.

Helen: Oh, Michael! How is he? I've been meaning to call him.

David: Oh, well, he's fine. He said you might possibly be able to help me with an article I'm writing.

Helen: If I can, sure, what's it about?

Now let's try it the other way round. Helen is frightened but David is listening and attending to her child

David: Hello, is that Helen Roxborough?

Helen: Yes.

David: Hi, I'm David Montgomery. Michael Davies said you were the best person I could talk to about an article I'm writing.

Helen: Oh?

David: Yes, he said when he came to you, you'd been really very helpful.

Helen: That's nice. So what's it about?

This is a very simplified version of an opening to a phone call. It's not to be copied verbatim. It's not a script! The intention is to show you how, by listening from a place of harmony, the tone of your voice will give the words a different feel and intention, and will help the listener to feel safe at every moment. You help *them* to listen to *you* from a place of harmony, not of fear. Secondly, because you are at ease with yourself, you'll really be listening to them, instead of being preoccupied with your own fears!

The biggest excuse given for not doing this is time! But how much time do we waste by avoiding people, by justifying why we're abrupt, or annoyed, because the other person didn't hear us? Are we terrified they'll take us over if we're more open? Helen hasn't said yes to helping David yet! Maybe she will, maybe she won't. But if Helen and

David have at least given each other the opportunity to be heard, the exchange will have been of value, whatever the final outcome. Both will put the phone down feeling they've made real contact with another human being. The next call they take or make will contain within it the reverberations of this conversation. They'll feel better about themselves and have recognized how their own state of harmony both affects them and those around them. The chain reaction grows!

As we've seen, when people meet each other, the people who meet first are the children inside. The frightened child is on guard, hypersensitive to the energy coming from another person. Each child will be waiting for the other to come out of hiding. If neither is prepared to risk it, the meeting will be sterile!

We will shortly start examining how to get in touch with your own frightened child in a very practical way, using your imagination. But even now you can begin to listen to the child in each and every person you meet and start to talk to them as if they were that friend you had your best ever conversation with. It doesn't matter whether the person is your boss, someone who's working for you or a stranger on the phone, each of them needs and deserves to be heard. The crucial thing is that you are listening to them from a place inside you without fear.

In the next section we'll be exploring not only your child but also the emotional and vocal range that every single person on this planet is capable of achieving. In less time than you think, you'll find your voice has changed – with a little help from the exercises we're going to do together – into something which is open and free and expresses the person who's been waiting to be heard for most of your life. You will begin to feel you truly belong to the world you live in and that you can make a difference to other people's lives just by talking to them from the heart. The title of this book is *Just Talk to Me*. Deep down inside, that's all anyone is asking you to do. And the part of them that's asking is their child.

CHAPTER SIX

FIT TO SPEAK

As I've said, talking is the movement of emotional energy which changes the emotional and physical state of the listener and of the speaker.

You're also an organized energy system which wants and needs to function in harmony. If you're out of harmony, either physically, emotionally or both, your 'instrument' won't work properly and the tunes and melodies you try to play will be discordant and painful to listen to and your 'message' will be muddled. What's worse, the people you're talking to will 'switch off'!

Also, if you as a person are unable to express yourself fully and clearly, without fear, you will only add to the confusion and fear of those around you.

If you're like the majority of people in this world, you were born in a natural state of harmony and equilibrium, as already mentioned. Your voice worked from the moment you took your first breath. You were born 'fit to speak'. Hopefully, both emotionally and physically there was no 'impediment'. But, as I've described, certain things along the way have affected this natural ability to fulfil your potential.

Yet the potential is still there, waiting to happen. What I hope to do is to give you the means to rediscover it!

Habits of a lifetime cannot be changed in a day. Nor can they be changed by just thinking about them. You, your child and your body need to develop again this instinctive knowledge from your past. The advantage you have is that it won't be new to you. You did it before and can do it again!

VOCAL STAMINA

You use your voice every day, probably taking it totally for granted, except maybe when you have a sore throat or a cold! Yet more than likely, you expect it to magically come alive when it's needed to speak to a group of people. Now, is that realistic? If, say, you were an athlete, would you assume that because you walk about a bit every day, all you need to do is jump up and down and do a few deep breathing exercises just before the big race? No, of course not, because to do something really strenuous and emotionally demanding, you need to be really fit. You need to have a carefully planned training programme, working your muscles up to peak performance level. You also need a carefully planned emotional strategy to be sure you believe you can win!

An actor who is planning to play Shakespeare's Hamlet would need to do exactly the same. The rehearsal process is not just about getting everyone moving around the stage without bumping into the furniture or each other! The most crucial part of the process is to unlock that part of the actor who is already the character they're going to play. (Actors don't play other people, they explore facets of themselves, which is exactly what we all do when we speak to other people.) Actors need to be emotionally available, so that the words they're saying touch them and move them as if they were their own.

Yet I guarantee they'll also be working on their body and their voice to make sure they're fit enough to carry their role. They wouldn't want their 'instrument' to let them down.

You may well say to me, 'Just talking to people is not the same as playing Hamlet.' Well, I hate to tell you this – it can all too easily be exactly the same!

Bearing in mind you probably won't be doing it every day, if you were to speak to an audience of 3,000 people for 20 minutes, that's as tough as Hamlet is for an actor. Remember, Hamlet doesn't do all the talking and he can have rests when he's off-stage! In your case you'd be the only one up there talking!

If you were giving an interview or being interviewed for 15 minutes live on network television for the first time, that's also as tough as Hamlet. If you were in a meeting and trying to save your company from going to the wall and had to justify why it shouldn't, knowing if you fail, you and 1,000 others will all be out of work, that's as tough as Hamlet!

What I'm saying is, if you're really committed to what you're saying, if you're speaking honestly and from the heart, you should be exhausted by the effort you've put in. If you've done it with conviction, you'll have expressed an awful lot of energy. Speaking to a group of people places incredible demands on your body. If you do it well, you'll be compensated by a wonderful feeling of elation, a genuine feeling of satisfaction of a job well done, a knowledge that you have reached out to your audience and really been heard.

Exercises to strengthen your physical and vocal ability are necessary for two main reasons. Firstly, speaking to more than one person requires a greater vocal stamina, especially when you're doing all the talking for 20 minutes! Secondly, you need to be absolutely certain that when you get up there you're ready to use the surge of adrenalin that comes with standing in front of a large number of people.

Just imagine you were asked to ride a racehorse in a big race when all you'd ever ridden before was a very docile pony. You know that if you were really fit and prepared you would have more chance of staying on the horse and even winning the race. If you weren't fit and ready, you'd either be crazy to get on the horse in the first place or totally freaked as it raced away. Adrenalin is the racehorse! If you plan to get up and speak, be assured it will be there and you'll have to get on it and be ready to fly. Remember, though, most jockeys stay on, most of the time. So can you, with a little preparation!

Every actor I know gets nervous, or, as they say, 'psyched up'.

They need the energy from the adrenalin to do the job.

Whether you're speaking to five people, 1,000 or 10,000, the essential energy needed will be the same. The only difference is you'll be using more of it when there are more people. (Not much more, because you need quite a bit just to speak well to five people.) This doesn't mean to say you'll need to shout – what it does mean is you need to be fitter than you are at the moment.

So how fit do you think you are? Come on, be honest!

The idea of getting fit can be alarming and you're possibly thinking, 'What's the point, it all seems too difficult!' The good news is that most of the muscles you'll be working on are very small and respond very quickly to the exercises I'll be giving you. All you'll need to do is just gently tickle them back into life. After each exercise you'll notice a difference. Really!

The bad news is, these muscles go to sleep again really quickly. They shrivel up in a matter of hours! What I'll be asking you to do is to gently build up their strength, so that they'll take longer to fall asleep, but get quicker at waking up. By becoming more aware of them and appreciating the difference they can make to how you speak, you'll enjoy using them more often and feel more and more secure that they're there for you whenever you need them.

EMOTIONS

The other crucial part of getting in shape to speak is learning how to express your feelings without fear. Three deep breaths before you go into a speaking situation is great. But if that's all you've done to prepare emotionally, then you are going to have more than a few problems when you start to open your mouth!

To unlock your emotions, we'll need to explore your ability to relax, to let go. Both you and your child need to be feeling emotionally and physically at ease, for your physical state is affected by your emotions and vice versa. As they're interconnected, so too are the exercises.

Always remember, being in harmony is not about being a floppy heap on the floor, but about enjoying a feeling of confident well-being, with your energy available and ready to meet the demands of talking to anyone.

Now, to do the work you're going to do, you have to believe you are worth it. Your child has to believe they're worth it too! I already believe in both of you! Coming this far has shown a commitment to wanting to improve the quality of an enormous chunk of your life. You've already shown you're prepared to make an effort to reach people and be heard.

I hope by now you're now more aware of the amazing untapped potential that's ready and waiting to happen. Knowing you are really being heard again will make an incredible difference to you. You'll feel empowered in every single aspect of your life.

Relaxed? Of Course I'm Relaxed!

We're going to start with a relaxation exercise to get in touch with your breathing. You'll need your breath to power your words. We'll also be getting in touch with your child. They'll be helping you to use the emotional energy you've been waiting to express.

Everything you're going to do I've done with most of my clients. If at any time you feel the need to stop or rest, please do so. This is for you to do in your own time at your own pace. Remember, there is no hurry. Allow yourself time to enjoy this new journey as you rediscover your true voice.

Virtually everyone I have worked with is convinced they're relaxed. They'll sit there in a tight ball in a slight state of what I've already called 'fight or flight' and firmly believe they're relaxed. Most of us, most of the time, carry enormous amounts of tension in our bodies and stress in our minds and accept it as normal.

However, most of us also have ways in which we allow ourselves to start to let go. Perhaps it's a drink, sitting in a favourite chair, listening to a favourite piece of music, or maybe it's going to the movies or a football match, or even engaging in strenuous exercise! Whatever your chosen trigger, you decide when to allow yourself to let go, just a little, the excess energies which the stresses and strains of your daily life can cause.

I'm sure by now you're aware that relaxation comes from within, from how you're feeling about yourself and the world you live in. But what stops you from feeling either safe enough or worthy enough to just pause for a moment and release what you're holding on to? Giving yourself permission is not always that easy, especially when you start thinking about being ready to get up and talk!

What we're going to be doing is taking what you already do a stage further. To achieve the results I'm hoping for, I'll be asking you to let your imagination run free. At times you may feel silly doing some of the exercises. But you have the advantage that nobody can see you! They might occasionally be able to hear you! But better that you prepare yourself in comparative privacy than embarrassing yourself and others when you try and give a speech or talk in a major meeting!

For virtually all the exercises I'm going to take you through, I want you to get into the habit of breathing through your mouth at all times and to feel the connection between the air around you and the air in your body. This has to become a habit for when you get up and talk. Breathing through your nose cuts you off from your connection with those you're talking to. You also can't get the air in quickly enough when you really need it! The amount of air you should be using to speak to a group of people for any length of time is enormous!

I've decided to put all of the lying down exercises together. This doesn't mean to say they should be done in one big block! Nor does it mean you don't begin the vocal exercises at the same time. I'll explain as we go along when it's best to do them.

- For your first few times through only do the 'Letting Go' and the first two exercises. When you feel really comfortable with them you can move on to the rest.
- Always remember to do the 'Letting Go' before you do anything else.
- Try and get to know the stages well so that you don't keep having to look at the book!
- If you feel brave enough, let someone else read them to you or put them on tape yourself.
- Always allow yourself the time to do each part without rushing.

If you go through them carefully, you'll remember them in no time!

LETTING GO

This first exercise will take about 20 minutes to do properly. In time you will be able to complete it in a matter of minutes, but not yet! Try not to rush it at the beginning, otherwise you'll never discover how relaxed you could really be. A little thought for you and your child – try not to run before you can walk!

Make some space on the floor so that you can lie down without bumping into anything. If you've got a belt on, loosen it. Ideally, none of your clothes should be tight fitting, especially around the waist.

Lie on your back on the floor with a book, about as thick as this one, under your head. Bring your knees up until your feet are flat on the floor and the small of your back is able to touch the ground without you forcing it down. Cross your arms over your chest for a moment to spread your shoulder blades. Bring your arms back and rest your left hand on the floor beside you (or, for now, hold the book!) Now, put the palm of your right hand below your tummy button, allowing the thumb to rest above. Now, imagine your back is gently spreading and sinking into the floor.

Relax your jaw. Remember to *breathe through your mouth*.

Start to become aware of the sounds in the room. What can you hear? Listen to each sound in turn. Now listen to the sounds outside the room. Listen to each sound in turn. What can you hear?

As you listen, become aware of your breathing. Don't change it, but feel the connection between the sounds you're hearing and how, if at all, they affect the air passing over your lips and down into your lungs. Feel the sensation of the air passing back out again, effortlessly.

See whether you can imagine the air coming into your lungs and going on down to where your right hand is. Don't force it, just imagine. Breathe out and in five or six times.

Now (when you can), close your eyes and start to feel a sense of relaxation and tranquillity. Imagine the air moving through your body from the inside. See if you can relax every part of your body, as you start to connect to your breathing.

Imagine as the air comes into you it moves on through to a particular part of your body. Imagine each part of your body being touched by the breath, releasing any tensions it may find.

Allow three breaths to go to each part of your body, easing the tensions just a little bit more each time, before you move on.

Breathe gently through your mouth as you imagine the air going to your toes

Breathe gently as you imagine the air going to the base of your feet

Breathe gently as you imagine the air going to your ankles

imagine the air going to your calves

imagine the air going to your knees

imagine the air going to your thighs

the air going to your bottom

the air going to your pelvis

the air going to your tummy

going to your lower back

going to your chest

                                    going to your upper back
                                        to your shoulders
                                        to your arms
                                        to your elbows
                                        to your forearms
                                        your wrists
                                        your fingers
                                        the back of your neck
                                        your throat
                                        your jaw
                                        your tongue
                                        your face
                                        your eyes
                                        the top of your head

Feel, as you continue to breathe, how the air is now moving more freely to every part of your body, moving you towards your natural state of harmony and well-being. Be aware of the release in the muscles of your tummy, of how much easier it is to breathe than before.

Remain where you are for as long as you're comfortable. Enjoy the sensation of feeling an effortlessness in every part of your being.

This is a gentle general relaxation which you can use at any time to bring yourself back into equilibrium. The more often you do this exercise, the easier it will be for you to talk from your natural place of harmony.

CHOICES
What next?

- If you feel content with what you've done, you can pause now until another time.
- If you want to liven yourself up again, you can turn to the beginning of the next chapter and gently start to connect with the power of your body to make sound. Remember both sections are interconnected. Choose the order which works for you. Follow your feelings!
- If you choose to get up now, do so very slowly, don't rush. Ideally, roll onto your side before you try to stand up.
- Or you can choose to move on and begin to ...

IMAGINE

What we're going to be doing now is to use your imagination a little more. Children are brilliant at this and so, somewhere inside you, are you! When you speak to other people, you speak in thoughts and images, using words. By reawakening your natural ability to imagine, thought by thought, breathing between each one, feeling the words and experiencing the emotions they carry, you'll transform your ability to paint pictures with words when you speak to other people. When you next give a speech you'll be able to live and feel the words you're saying instead of resorting to faked emotion – or, to put it another way, 'bad acting'.

I'd like you to do these 'imaginations' in the order they're in for now. Later, you can pick and choose which ones work best for you at different times. But please, only do them after you've done the 'Letting Go'.

Allow your right hand to rest on your tummy as before. See if you can keep the air flowing in and out of you, whatever the words make you feel. Try and keep your breathing open and free. Try not to lock up your breath. If you do start to feel things as we go through, allow them to happen. Allow them to be expressed.

Finally, don't try and do more than two of these exercises in any one session. Give them time. There is no hurry!

1. YOUR SPECIAL PLACE

As you rest back into the floor, I want you to imagine...
A place where you feel totally safe.
Totally at peace.
Where you don't have to be anything.
You don't have to impress anyone.
You don't have to be charming.
You don't have to talk.
A place where you can truly let go.

Wherever it is, I want you to go there now, in your mind's eye.
Breathe gently, as you feel and experience this special place you are in.
Are you standing or sitting or lying down?
Are you inside or outdoors?
What can you see?
Look around you.
Is it light or dark?
See and sense the quality of light.
Is it warm or is it cool?
Can you feel any wind on your face?
What can you smell?
Allow yourself to feel the pleasure of what you're experiencing as you breathe into your special place.
All the cares in your life are a distant dream as you enjoy your own special place. Breathe into the feeling of this magical place, your place, your safe space.

This place you're in is yours.

It belongs to you.

It's real, in your mind's eye.

Just as real as any memory you may have.

It's your creation.

Breathe into your safe and secure place.

Your magical place.

You can come here whenever you wish.

Know it will always be here, waiting for you to return, whenever
  you wish. Whenever you feel tense or uncomfortable, in less than
  a moment, you can return here, return to your special place, to
  your safe and magical place, which belongs to you and you alone.

All I ask is you remember to come here.

Choose to say goodbye to your magical place for now, or, if you
wish, you can stay here as we meet someone you already know.

2. LEARNING TO LISTEN AGAIN

As you rest back into the floor with your right hand on your
  tummy, be in your magical safe place again.

I want you to imagine there's a child who's been hidden from the
  world, who's been in hiding, waiting for someone to come and
  listen to them.

They're slowly walking towards you.

They look just like you did when you were their age.

Can you see them? See them in your mind's eye?

What are they wearing? How do they look?

Do they like this magical place you've created?

Look gently into their eyes.

Are they pleased to see you or are they still a little sad?

They want to tell you something.

Do you know, can you guess?

They're upset, but they're frightened to tell.
Is it safe? Is it safe to tell? Will you listen?
Are you there for them, as they start to tell?
Breathe gently with them, as they start to tell you what's been
  hurting them for so long.

They wish it hadn't happened.
Even after all this time they wish it had never happened.
They did the best they could to cope on their own.
There was no one they could tell.
Their way of dealing with it helped them survive.
But they're still hurting.
It felt so unfair, so wrong, so unkind.
They know they didn't deserve it.
They tried to deal with it on their own, they tried to work it out.
They tried to pretend it didn't happen.
But they still remember.
It's been a secret for so long.
A secret they swore to themselves they would keep forever.
No one was ever to know.
But it still hurts.
It still feels so unjust.
It wasn't their fault.
It still hurts.
They've never ever talked about it.
Not to anyone.
But they wish they could.
Just once.
They wish more than anything to find someone who they can truly
  trust, who will stop whatever they're doing and really listen.
Not to laugh at them, not to make them feel stupid.
Not to judge them as an awful human being.
To show them some real compassion.
To reassure them and promise them, if it ever happens again,

they'll help them deal with it in a better way.
A way that won't leave them feeling so lonely.
Please will you listen?
Please can they tell?

Are you listening?
Can you hear them?
Can you bring yourself to say you really feel compassion for how
    they feel?
Can you reassure them that if it does happen again, you'll be there
    for them to help to deal with it in a better way?
One that won't leave them feeling so lonely?

You know who they are.
They're the best friend you ever had.
Even though they're so young, they've done all they can to protect
    you from the cruelties of the world.
They're that part of you, the part who's been so frightened, so ter-
    rified, for so many years.
The part of you who's been so hurt and sad that no one has lis-
    tened.
They've longed to find someone whom it was safe to tell.
Someone who would help them to release all the energy that's been
    locked up inside and got in the way of having a really happy life.
They want to feel again that wonderful feeling of harmony and
    safety.
The one they had when they were very young.
They need to know you'll be there for them.
You'll help them to make it all alright.
They need to know it's safe to come out and play again.
It's safe to be loved.

Know that you're not alone with what you may be feeling.
Be elated: finally you've been heard.

If you're feeling tearful, know the emotion you've held inside has
finally been released.

Feel happy that at last you can look after each other on the next
stage of your life. No one can ever hurt either of you again.

Your secret isn't a secret anymore.

It's lost its power over you.

There is nothing to be afraid of ever again.

There is no more to fear.

You will survive, with a little help from your young friend.

You can finally talk to the part of you that knows better than you
do how to find your feeling of harmony and equilibrium that's
eluded you for so long.

Gently reach out your hand to this very special person in your life.

Feel their hand in yours, knowing you will face the world together
from now on.

3. YOUR FIRST MEETING

As you relax back with your right hand on your tummy, I want you
to imagine a day in your life when you were a young child, a day
when you were really happy, when everything made you feel good
and made you laugh out loud with glee. See if you can be there in
your mind's eye. Breathe into the feeling. See the people around
you. Picture it in all its detail. Listen to the people around you.
Hear the sounds in all their detail. Feel the people around you. Feel
the energy passing in and out and through you. Feel what you felt
like, all over again. Stay with that feeling and breathe into it several times.

Move the feeling into your right hand and hold it there.

Hold the feeling, while you search out another day.

Put your left hand on your tummy as you remember a day when you were still a child, a day when you felt very frightened, very hurt, very rejected, when the people you loved didn't seem to be there for you. Be there in your mind's eye. Breathe into the feeling. See the people around you. Picture it in all its detail. Listen to the people around you. Hear the sounds in all their detail. Feel the people around you. Feel the energy passing in and out and through you. Feel what you felt, all over again. Breathe into the feeling several times. Gently move the feeling into your left hand.

Lie there for a moment, knowing in your left hand is a very sad part of you and in your right hand a very happy part of you. Gently bring your hands towards each other and rest them on your tummy. Allow the right hand to stroke the left hand. Allow the happy part of you to stroke the sad part of you as you all breathe together, as the happy child eases the pain of the frightened child, taking the pain and letting it go.

Finally rest both your hands back onto your tummy and breathe.

4. THE SOUND OF LIGHT

As you relax back, I want you to imagine you are walking alone through a dark forest.

You are younger than you are now.

You are tired and lonely.

You are carrying on your back a heavy load.

All the burdens you have carried all through your life are contained in a huge sack you're struggling to hold on to.

Way ahead you see a light.

As you move towards the light, you see that it's coming from a log cabin.

As you move closer, you can hear the sound of voices.

You walk up the steps towards the front door of the cabin.

The sounds become clearer.

You recognize the voices of people you know.

You knock on the door, which gently opens.

There in front of you are all the people you have ever met in your life.

They call you by your name as they greet you.

You move from person to person.

Each is smiling at you, each is pleased to see you as they say your name and say hello.

Walking towards you out of the crowd are the two most important people in your life.

The two people who have helped you the most.

They reach out their hands.

Each holds one of yours as they say your name.

You feel their warm energy passing into you, as they lead you through a small door.

As you pass through this door, you bend down a little.

As you bring your head up, you find yourself in a room full of lighted candles.

The candles flicker and glisten.

In the corner of the room you see a large golden chest lying open.

Your two special friends guide you gently towards the chest.

They reach behind you and carefully lift off the huge sack you are carrying on your back.

You feel the relief as the weight falls from your back.

They help you take it and put it into the chest.

You close the lid of the golden chest and lock it with a padlock.

You take the key in your left hand.

Your two friends then lead you through another small door.

Again, you have to bend down to pass through.

As you pass through the doorway you bring your head up to find yourself in a room of perfect white light.

Standing smiling at you is the one person who has done the most to help you in your life, the person who made all the difference.

You have a distant memory as you see who it is.

They are the part of you that's older and wiser than you are now.

The quiet voice you occasionally hear, the one who is always there for you, quietly caring for you, supporting you and loving you, maybe at a distance, but always there.

They say your name as they smile and move towards you.

You look into each other's eyes.

You see the face of your future.

You stand for a moment, hand in hand as you feel the energy you always feel when you're with them.

Gently they lead you to a white platform and guide you to lie down.

They gently take the key from your left hand and promise to look after it always.

As you lie down, you can feel the lightness of your body as the room begins to melt away.

The energy that moves in and out and through you is the most brilliant white light.

Pure and clear.

Cleansing and purifying every cell in your body.

You become the light.

The sound you can hear is the sound of the white light.

Vibrating every cell in your body.

Your energy is moving in perfect harmony with the energy around and in and through you.

You are total harmony in the white light and the white sound.

Perfectly in harmony once more.

5. TALKING TO ANOTHER'S CHILD

As you relax I want you to imagine that in front of you is someone who you do not like, someone who has hurt you in the past.

Imagine you are talking to them about why they are so unpleasant to you.

Instead of talking to that part of them they usually present to you, you're listening to the voice behind their unkind words.

You're hearing the voice of their frightened child.

You hear and see them for the first time.

When you speak to them you use your most genuine and open voice, the voice connected to your own child.

You feel the energy from you go into their child as you speak.

You ask the child what's hurting them and why they're always so angry.

You wait patiently and listen very carefully to what they say.

If they're evasive, ask them again, more gently than before, showing them you won't hurt them.

You're there for them and you will listen to what they need to say.

You treat them with the same compassion as you would any frightened child who needed to be heard and helped.

6. THE WISE CHILD

As you relax, I want you to imagine it's dark and you're sitting round a fire late in the evening with 100 members of your tribe.

You're one of the wise ones who has been asked to speak to the tribe.

You have no fear.

You have spoken before and will do so again.

You are loved and respected by every member of the tribe.

Sitting close to the ground are the children of the tribe.

Two of them, a boy and a girl, are your grandchildren.

See them smiling at you.

See the tribe watching and waiting with a glow of anticipation.

Part of the ritual in your tribe is to look and breathe, taking in everyone around the fire, before you speak.

You do not have to think of what you're going to say.

You know the words and thoughts will be there for you when you come to speak.

All you need do is to feel and sense the whole group, just as you would if you were going to speak to your best friend.

Every single one of them is your best friend.

They're a part of you.

You're a part of them.

The energy of the tribe flows in and out and through you.

Your energy flows in and out and through them.

You breathe out and in five times.

You feel the energy inside you and all around you.

You feel the energy of the tribe.

You can hear the frightened child in all of them.

You know there is something that needs to be expressed by you to bring the tribe back into perfect harmony.

As you breathe and feel the energy, prepare to make your 'sound', an expression of your 'body sound', an expression of your energy, connecting you to the tribe.

This is the sound which comes out of you before you speak.

This sound is repeated like a chant, until the whole tribe is connected to you and you with them.

The sound starts as a hum which opens into 'arh' sound.

It's the sound of the wise child in you.

In your own time, make your sound.

Gently repeat the sound.

Feel the sound move through your body.

Feel the sound vibrating your whole body.

Feel the sound bringing your whole body into harmony.

See and feel the tribe support you in the sound you're making, for as long and as loud as you feel it is needed.

If there's any other sound you wish to express, make it now.

7. What Do I Like About...?

Standing on a stage, in your mind's eye, is someone you truly
   admire as a speaker.
Think what it is about them you really like, what part of you most
   identifies with them.
As you watch them speak, hear their child.
Hear their rhythms and tones.
Start to feel their rhythm.
Start to feel their tones.
Start to feel how they feel.
Imagine you're moving as they move.
Breathe as they breathe, as you start to speak.
As you continue to speak, allow those parts of them that don't feel
   comfortable to float away, as you continue with those parts of
   them that do.

Be sure you've already been working through the vocal exercises
before you try this next imagination. It will only make complete sense
when you've worked right through the book. But don't let that stop
you!

8. Today's the Day

It's morning and you've just woken. Today's the day you are going
to give a major speech to 3,000 people. Television cameras will be
there from the major networks. They'll be sending your message
out to 10 million people, who will be watching and listening to
everything you say, live as you say it.
   You slept well. You're excited at the opportunity to talk from the
heart about something that really matters to you. You're feeling a

wonderful flow of energy through your body. You're glad it's there, ready to be used. You need this movement of energy for what you're going to be doing today. Today you will be 'a mover of energy'. You feel in harmony with yourself and what you are going to do. You are totally focused on helping an audience by expressing their fears and moving them to a place of harmony within themselves. Your purpose is to move the audience to do something important: to change the way they feel and think for the sake of the greater good. You have been chosen to speak on behalf of others, whose voices need to be heard. You are speaking for them, you are their voice. Their energy is passing through you, helping to give you the power you need to help them back into harmony. No longer does your child feel afraid. They're excited. They know they'll be there, helping you to speak to the child inside each and every person who'll be watching and listening. They'll be there with you, listening to the audience, making sure that every thought you express is understood, allowing you to feel safe in the knowledge that you will truly be heard.

You wash and dress in your usual way but with an extra feeling of well-being.

You very gently start to hum, moving the sound around your body. All the preparation you've done is there in the sound you are making. You feel your power. You feel your energy in the form of sound. You continue to work through your vocal exercises; very relaxed, very easy. You've done them many times before, you'll do them many times again. They're now part of your daily routine of moving your energy through your body, of bringing you back into harmony. You enjoy the sounds you're making. Hearing your sound focuses you on your ability to hear the needs in others and respond.

You have your usual breakfast – just enough to take away any hunger pains, but not so much that the blood goes to your stomach. You don't have an extra cup of coffee – you don't need your energy to be moving any faster. You give yourself the time and space to go through the whole speech, word for word. You feel confident, knowing your breathing and your mouth are working perfectly, ready to support you when you deliver the speech to your audience.

Your journey to the venue is gentle and easy. You arrive in good time. People you know are already there. They wish you well. You say thank you. They seem nervous. But what they're really feeling is over-excited – excited at what you'll achieve for them and for everyone who listens to what you have to say. There's someone there who occasionally in the past has made you tense. Their energy is confused and they send out messy vibes. Today you are so focused that your energy moves towards and through them, shifting them into a place of harmony they're not used to. It's as if the energy you are giving out washes away their bad vibes.

Your child feels a momentary fear as the adrenalin starts to flow through your body. You knew it was coming, you've been waiting for it to happen, and you place your hand on your tummy to calm and reassure your child that all is well. You no longer have any secrets to hide. You are both safe. Your child's fears turn to pleasure and excitement.

So many people say, 'Hi.' Their energy passes through you without any need to block them out. You ride their waves of energy. Occasionally you hum, very quietly under your breath, staying in tune, rebalancing your energy. You continue to be in touch with who you really are and what you're going to say.

You find somewhere where you can be quiet for a few moments – maybe it's the loo or a side corridor. You take a moment to return to your safe space, to remember again who you really are, to centre your energy. With your child, you take a moment to remember what you hope to achieve together. You have spoken brilliantly before and you will speak brilliantly today. You've prepared what you want to say, what you *really* want to say. You wish yourself well and move towards the hall.

You can feel the energy as you walk into the hall. You know that by speaking to the people gathered to hear you you will make a difference in their lives. You will help them to understand the world they live in a little more. You will help to release their fears, the energy that's blocked inside them. You will express your energy into them and help to bring them nearer to their state of harmony and equilibrium. You will shift the energy in the hall by the power of your voice. The energy will be moved by you from fear and anger into harmony. You can hear and feel their fears, but you yourself have none. You will be speaking as if to a girl of 13, someone who's very intelligent, but not yet worldly. You won't assume she understands; you'll check whether she's following your words. It will be a perfect conversation. You feel the responsibility you've been given. But it isn't a burden.

The moment has come and you're being introduced. The energy in you is moving even faster, ready to be used. Your hand rests on your tummy as you make contact with your child, ready for you both to speak. The wave of energy you know and love is lifting you up as you walk towards the lectern. You place your notes down as you rehearsed. You look around the hall and take everyone in as you breathe with them. You feel their energy. All eyes are focused on you. All the children are focused on you. You breathe in their energy and begin your conversation. Very slowly, you say your first few words, just as you would if only one frightened child were sitting there, a child you wanted to reach with your words and emotions. In the hall, each child is hearing you talking to them and them alone. Everything feels as though it's in slow motion as you breathe between each thought. Each thought touches you again as if for the first time. You listen to what you've just said, with the audience. It touches you as it touches them. All of you are in the same moment, sharing the same feelings. You become one being, expressing feelings and emotions that you all share, joined by a web of interconnected energy. They know you are really talking to them and nothing else matters. The ritual exchange of words and emotions between one human being and another is being re-experienced. Whatever emotions you feel about what you're saying will be expressed as you feel them. Nothing will be imposed, nothing will be faked. Whatever you feel now about what you're saying, be it anger, frustration or passion, all will be expressed.

As you move towards your conclusion you know you have been heard. You know you shared with your audience the energy in the room as you moved them towards a state of well-being. The audience were just as much a part of the conversation as you were. It was shared by you all.

The audience, as one, send to you a wave of sound in the form of applause, sending back to you their transformed energy. You can hear the difference you've made. They give you their energy, their sound. The exchange and transformation of energy has been fulfilled for you all. You have brought everyone closer to their natural state of harmony and helped them to move nearer to their place in the world.

'Today's the Day' will only make complete sense when you've worked through the whole book. But, as before, don't let that stop you doing it!

As you will quickly realize, this next imagination is very similar, but it will prepare you for a very different environment.

9. Could We Have an Interview?

As you relax back, again I want you to imagine you're the most wonderful speaker, praised for your honesty, your directness, your openness, your warmth and the enormous pleasure people get from hearing you. You are known for your ability to reach and speak to everyone. Young or old, everyone feels you're really talking to them. You are your wise child.

It's morning and you've just woken. Today you are going to be interviewed live on a major television network. You'll be subjected to a probing interview by one of the most controversial broadcasters on national television. Ten million people will be watching and listening to everything you say, live as you say it.

You slept well. You're excited at the opportunity to talk from the heart about something that really matters to you. You're feeling a wonderful flow of energy through your body. You're glad it's there, ready to be used. You need this movement of energy for what you're going to be doing today. Today you will be 'a mover of energy'. You feel in harmony with yourself and what you are going to do. You are totally focused on talking about what really matters to you, open to discussing the fear and anger expressed by the interviewer on behalf of the viewers and moving them towards a place of harmony within themselves, changing the way they feel and think for the sake of the greater good. You have been chosen to speak on behalf of others, whose voices need to be heard. You are speaking for them, you are their voice. Their energy is passing through you, helping to give you the power you need to help them back into harmony.

No longer does your child feel afraid. They're excited. They know they'll be there, helping you to speak to the child inside each and every person who'll be watching and listening. They'll be there with you, listening to the audience, making sure that every thought you express is understood, allowing you to feel safe in the knowledge that you will truly be heard.

You wash and dress in your usual way but with an extra feeling of well-being. You very gently start to hum, moving the sound around your body. All the preparation you've done is there in the sound you are making. You feel your power. You feel your energy in the form of sound. You continue to work through your vocal exercises. Very relaxed, very easy. You've done them many times before, you'll do them many times again. They're now part of your daily routine of moving your energy through your body, of bringing you back into harmony. You enjoy the sounds you're making. Hearing your sound focuses you on your ability to hear the needs in others and to respond.

You have your usual breakfast – just enough to take away any hunger pains, but not so much that the blood goes to your stomach. You don't have an extra cup of coffee; you don't need your energy to be moving any faster. You give yourself the time and space to go through each major point of your story's structure and your triggers. You feel confident, knowing your breathing and your mouth are working perfectly, ready to support you as you begin to talk to the person interviewing you.

Your journey to the studio is gently and easy. You arrive at the reception in good time. You are friendly to the people who greet you, even if they seem tense or detached. Their energy feels confused and they send out messy vibes, but today you are so focused that your energy moves toward and through them, shifting them into a place of harmony they're not used to. Your child feels a momentary fear as the adrenalin starts to flow through your body, but you knew it was coming, you've been waiting for it to happen, and you place your hand on your tummy to calm and reassure your child. All is well. You no longer have any secrets to hide. You are both safe. No one can hurt you. Your child's fears turn to pleasure and excitement. All is well. Occasionally you hum, very quietly under your breath, staying in tune, rebalancing your energy.

Someone comes and takes you to a room nearer the studio. As you walk, they explain what's going to happen. They go through with you what the subject of the interview will be and what you're likely to be asked. Their energy passes through you. You also feel the energy of those you pass. You ride their waves of energy as you listen to what you're being told. You're taken into a room and told someone will come for you a few minutes before you go 'on air'.

You take a moment to return to your safe space, to remember again who you really are, to centre your energy. You and your child take a moment to remember what you hope to achieve together. You have been interviewed before and you will be interviewed again. You know what you want to say – what you *really* want to say. You know that by speaking openly and honestly to the person interviewing you, as if they were your best friend, you will help them and the viewers to understand the world we live in a little more. You will help to release their fears, release the energy that's blocked inside them. You will express your energy and help to bring them nearer to their state of harmony and equilibrium. You will shift their energy by the power of your voice. The energy in the studio and in people's homes will be moved from fear and anger into a state of harmony as you help them to release their fears for their future. You continue to hum gently.

An assistant comes and finds you, telling you they'll take you into the studio when they go into a pre-recorded item. You pause and wait calmly, keeping in touch with your energy. You wish yourself well as you move towards the studio.

You're called into the studio. You feel the heat of the lights. You can feel the tension of a live programme going out all over the country. You continue to breathe easily as you're shown to your chair near the interviewer. A sound person puts a microphone on you, connecting your voice to the people you're going to be talking to. The adrenalin in the studio is immense. You get used to all the lights and all the attention. The interviewer smiles and greets you. They are affable but guarded, preparing themselves for what's to come. You can hear and feel their energy. You can hear and feel their child. They want to bring out what is important in what you have to say. You can feel the enormous pressure they are under to do their job well. You understand their needs and you respond with a smile and a 'hello'. You listen and watch everything that's happening. You and your child are excited by the energy. You have no fear. The interviewer says he will start with a particular question to introduce the subject. You're told they'll be coming to you in 30 seconds.

The moment has come and you're being introduced. Your energy is moving even faster, ready to be used. Your hand rests on your tummy as you connect again to that other part of you, ready for you both to speak. The wave of energy you know and love is lifting you up as the red light on your camera comes on. The eye of the camera is not cold. On the other side of the lens are the people you want and need to reach. The lens connects you to them. The microphone connects you to them. All eyes and ears are focused on you. All the children are focused on you. You breathe in their energy and begin your conversation.

The interviewer asks the first question. Their energy is very powerful. They're louder and more forceful than they were when they said hello. You allow your energy to respond. You listen carefully to what they're asking you, connecting their words to what you want to say. You look into their eyes as you would a dear friend and gently begin your reply.

You talk as if to a girl of 13, someone who is very intelligent, but not yet worldly. You won't assume she'll understand; you'll check whether she's following your words. It will be a perfect conversation. You feel the responsibility you've been given. But no burden. The child in each and every person watching at home is hearing you talking to them and them alone. Everything feels as though it's in slow motion as you breathe between each thought. Each thing you say touches you again as if for the first time. You listen to what you've just said, at the same moment as the interviewer and the viewer. It touches you as it touches them. All of you are in the same moment, sharing the same feelings. You become one being, expressing feelings and emotions that you all share, joined by a web of interconnected energy. They know you are really talking to them and nothing else matters. The ritual exchange of words and emotions between one human being and another is being re-experienced again several million times. Whatever emotions you feel about what you really want to say will be expressed as you feel them. Nothing will be imposed, nothing will be faked. This is what you feel now. Whether it be anger, frustration or fears for the future, all will be expressed.

The perfect conversation continues. As the interviewer asks you a probing question, you hear the pain they're expressing. You don't ignore it, but breathe as you allow you and your child to find the answer. You answer as honestly as you can – just as you would if a frightened child were sitting there – while remaining clear and focused on what you want to say. You remember, too, the 13-year-old girl who needs to hear and understand your answer. There is no hurry, as you explain what you want to say.

Now the interview is over. As the interviewer thanks you, you know you have been heard. You know you shared with the interviewer and the viewers the energy you all felt as you moved them towards a state of well-being. The viewers were just as much a part of the conversation as you were. It was shared by you all. You know you've made a difference. The exchange and transformation of energy has been fulfilled. You have brought everyone closer to their natural state of harmony and helped them to move nearer to their place in the world.

Each of these imaginations represents a different part of our work together. Each deserves to be done more than once! The more you repeat them, the more you'll move towards a deeper sense of who you really are and what you're really here to do and say. You'll also be laying the ghosts of your past finally to rest.

'Today's the Day' and 'Could We Have an Interview?' are of value not just for building your belief in your ability to give a major speech or give a television interview, but also to speak to any number of people at any time. Every time you share what you really care about with another person, it deserves the same respect as when you speak to 3,000 or 10 million.

10. A PHOTOGRAPH OF YOU

I'd like you to find a photograph of yourself taken when you were a young child, a photograph of you smiling genuinely into the lens with an open happy face.

When you've found one, I'd like you to stand in front of a mirror and hold the picture up next to your face. See whether when you look into the child's eyes you can copy their smile. Look deep into the child's eyes and allow yourself to take on the feeling they're sending out to you. See if you can move your face into exactly the same look and feel what the child is feeling.

Breathe into that feeling, until you know again what it was to be them. Feel the energy change in your body as you feel again their happiness. Put your hand on your tummy and feel where they are. Breathe into the feeling. In their innocence, they sent a message to the future, a message to remind you of who you really are.

LEARNING TO BREATHE AGAIN

The more in touch you are with your breathing, the more connected you'll be to your child. The physical connects you to the emotional. By working with these exercises and the imaginations at the same time, you'll really start to connect with the power within you to express what you want to say without fear.

Unlike any other exercises you may have done, with these you'll not only feel the difference, you'll *hear* the difference, every time you talk! You'll be reminded all through the day of how worthwhile these exercises really are.

They're not difficult. Honestly! I've designed them for people who don't want to do them! They're a basic set, which will give you the best results for the least amount of effort and will improve the quality of your voice more than you can imagine. I don't mind if you never do any other voice exercises (of which there are thousands) in your life, so long as you do the ones in this chapter and do them regularly and often. Also, remember to do the 'imaginations' too, as they'll add a magical dimension to everything we do together!

You'll discover for yourself which exercises have the greatest effect on your particular voice. I, for one, have to do the lips exercises the most, because when I'm feeling lazy, I manage to talk without using them at all! All I then get in response is, 'What? Eh? What did you say?'

In a short space of time, these exercises will become your vocal warm up to the day. Make them part of your personal trigger to speaking from the heart and you will be able to unlock your true voice every single time you talk.

Breathing through your Mouth

All through these exercises, I want you to remember, at all times, to breathe through your mouth. You are going to need to get into the habit of using a lot more air. Breathing through your nose just doesn't give you the level of access to your lungs that you need when you speak to a large group of people for any length of time.

Why is this? Firstly, because it takes too long! Imagine the process that goes on: you say a few words, close your mouth, close your throat, breathe in through your nose, open your mouth, open your throat and then you speak again.

Secondly, it helps to keep your throat open. Most people form their words at the back of a tight throat. This is just about OK in everyday conversation, but if you need to speak for longer and with more volume and power, you will wreck your throat. Words should be formed with an open throat, using the middle and front of your tongue and your lips, not the back of your tongue and your throat.

Finally, if you breathe through your nose, you cut yourself off from the people you're talking to while you sort out your air! Each time you say something else, you have to reconnect. That is very exhausting both for you and for those listening and, what's more, a waste of valuable energy.

I want you to develop as direct a connection as you possibly can between your lungs and the person you're talking to – between their child and your child. It will make sense as you do it. So please, start to breathe through your mouth.

THE EXERCISES

Remember, this is not a power workout. I'm not looking for the burn! It's about feeling the difference from the inside. When you go through these exercises for the first time, don't feel you have to do them all from beginning to end, in one go. Make sure you give yourself time to really experience each one in turn. Like anything, if you learn it properly the first time, it will stick in your memory. There's no point in rushing on. What I've prepared is the short version – you really can't make it any shorter! Soon you'll be able to do the exercises in the car or walking down the street – well, most of them! You'll very quickly discover which of these exercises should become part of your daily warm up. The more regularly you do them, the more quickly your voice will develop into the voice you've always wished you had!

1. GETTING CENTRED

Stand with your feet apart, nearly as wide as your shoulders. Check you're neither slumping forwards or backwards. Allow your head to float on your neck and shoulders. Now, relax your neck and shoulders. Move your top half backwards and forwards to be sure you're not using any muscles in your back or your front to support yourself. If the spine is in alignment it'll support you without your help. Imagine most of your body weight is in the region just below your tummy button. Unlock your knees by slightly bending them and feel the connection of your feet to the ground. Become aware of your breathing. Don't change it, just be aware of it. Begin to feel 'centred'. This is when your tummy region becomes the centre of your body. Many people allow their head or chest to be their 'centre'. They're not 'grounded' at all.

2. THE STRETCH

Now, gently stretch your left side, bringing your left arm over your head in a gentle arc, breathing all the time through your mouth. Be aware of the slight stretch in your rib-cage as you take in air.

Now to the right side. Remember to keep your knees slightly bent.

3. THE SHAKE OUT

Shake out your arms and legs, allowing your elbows and wrists, knees and ankles to be really floppy.

4. THE BARREL ROLL

Stand with your feet apart, arms relaxed by your side and knees slightly bent. Allow your head to roll forward and down. Let its weight take you on down, still rolling. Think about each vertebra moving, as you come to it, shifting one at a time. Imagine, as you go down, that you are falling over a barrel in front of you. Allow your arms and head to hang, don't hold on. Keep breathing.

Carry on down until your arms and head are just hanging there. Feel the release in your lower back. This area of your spine takes a great deal of stress, not just the weight of your body, but also the tension you carry.

Hang there for about 30 seconds. Go through your body, checking you're not holding on to any tension. Remember to breathe through your mouth with a relaxed jaw. This is incredibly relaxing for your spine.

Now gently come up again. Build back up, one vertebra on top of the next, leaving your head and arms hanging. The last thing you do is to bring your head slowly back up off your chest. Imagine you're a puppet with strings gently holding you up. Allow your head and shoulders to gently float on top of your body. Breathe through your mouth, with a relaxed jaw, your knees still slightly bent. Be aware of a new sense of release and relief as you take your rightful space.

Any time you feel you are 'locking up', do this exercise. It works!

5. FACES

Scrunch your face up, really tight and closed. Then make it really wide and open. Now, really long and 'yawny'. Move your lips every which way. Keep breathing. Blow lots of little kisses, real smackers, so the air really squeaks.

Relax the face and jaw. Bring your lips together, still really relaxed. Blow through them just like a horse. Let the lips be really floppy as they flap!

Most people carry a lot of tension in their jaw. This next exercise helps you to relax it a little more, without doing any damage. Forcing your mouth open and your jaw down is really bad for you and only adds to your tension. Nor should you attempt to move it from side to side, as that's something it was never designed to do!

6. JAWS

Relax the face and jaw and, breathing through your mouth, relax your arms by your side. Leaving the top half of your arms hanging loose, bend them at the elbow and gently clasp your hands together in front of your chin. Gently shake them towards and away from your chin, trying not to hit it!

Now move a little faster, keeping the rest of your body relaxed. Concentrate on the movement of your forearms – don't start to help with your head!

Now make an 'arh' sound, with an open throat, while still moving your arms.

Do this exercise for about 15 seconds. Feel the release in your jaw, which hopefully has been moving by itself.

BREATHING FROM THE DIAPHRAGM – THE POWERHOUSE

So, where's the diaphragm and what is it? Here I'll give you my version, which explains what the diaphragm does in a form that I can handle as an actor and hope will help you to achieve the results you need to speak well.

The diaphragm is a membrane between your internal organs and your lungs that almost cuts you in half just below the rib-cage. Using the large muscles around your tummy button, you are able to push this membrane up and squeeze the air out of your lungs. When you relax it, you release the pressure on your lungs, which, not being muscle, go back to their normal state, pulling air back into them through your mouth or nose. The big muscles, around and below your tummy button, the ones you think of as the tummy muscles, come into use in nearly everything you do, whether standing, walking, bending, lifting or going to the loo! However, their major role as far as I'm concerned is that they help you to breathe. They're the muscles you should be using most to push the air out of your lungs. Unfortunately, most people hardly use them at all to breathe! Instead they rely on tiny breaths using their upper chest muscles. This cuts them off from their child and their emotions.

These large muscles won't want to wake up immediately, particularly if they've been closed down for any length of time, as they probably have! You'll really have to be very gentle with them at first. You can be a little tougher on them later, when you've got the hang of it!

Before we begin to work with these big bruisers I want you to understand something which is at the core of much of the work you and I are going to do together. **You need to put the effort into breathing out, not into breathing in.**

What does this mean? Well, most people, especially when they get nervous, believe they have to pull air into their lungs before they can speak. Before they start, they'll take a big deep breath. They'll say a sentence and then, if they can manage it, take another huge lungful of air, usually through their nose, and then say the next thing. This is the quickest way to lock up your breathing! Actors, if they're any good, don't do this. They concentrate their effort into pushing the air out, over their vocal chords, to form the words in all their detail. Just like a spring that's been squashed down, when they relax their muscles, miraculously, in an instant, their lungs spring back and are full of air again. Wow! Just like that. Sounds easy? Well it is when you've got the knack. It also becomes very natural, believe me!

Deeper and fuller sounds need much more air. The low notes on a church organ need bucketfuls of air. The high piccolo notes need very little. As I'm hoping to persuade you to speak with more than a squeak, I need to get your lungs working harder!

Before you start these exercises, I'd ideally like you to have done the 'Letting Go', especially at the beginning

7. FEEL THE AIR

Find a straight-backed chair and sit in it, putting your bottom into the back of the chair, your feet flat on the floor, slightly apart. Make sure you haven't got anything tight around your waist. If you've got a belt on, loosen it. Allow your head to float and relax your neck and shoulders. Remember to breathe through your mouth, not your nose.

Become aware of your breathing. Don't change it, but feel the connection as the air passes over your lips and down into your lungs. Feel the sensation of it passing back out again.

Now, put your the palm of your hand below your tummy button, allowing the thumb to rest above. See if you can imagine the air coming into your lungs is going on down to where your hand is. Don't force it, just imagine.

Close your eyes and feel a sense of relaxation and tranquillity. Imagine the air moving through your body from the inside. See if you can relax every other part of your body as you start to connect to your breathing. Allow this to continue for a minute or so.

This next exercise is the big one. This is where you get to really feel what I'm talking about when I say we need to relearn how to put the effort into breathing out, **not** into breathing in!

8. THE BIG BLOW

I want you to breathe out through your mouth, as far as you can, then a little more. Really push the air out, using your tummy muscles, keeping your mouth and throat open.

Hold the air out, using only your tummy muscles, not your throat, until you feel the strong urge for air. Make sure your mouth and throat are open, then just let go. (If you need a trigger, imagine someone has just come into the room you haven't seen for ages and gasp.) Don't pull the air in. Your lungs should fill up with air by themselves. It won't be the deepest breath you've ever taken, but it will be enough.

The temptation will be to pull some extra air in, so that you feel you've done something. Don't be tempted!

Repeat this exercise twice more.

That's enough for now, this is just the beginning. I really don't want you to force this exercise. When you do it again, say, later today or tomorrow, begin to feel more and more that the effort is on the **out** breath, but none whatsoever on the **in** breath.

Don't expect to wake this muscle up in one session. It takes the longest to come to life, but once you've got the sense of what you are doing – effort on the out breath, then totally let go – everything else will fall into place.

A different approach with the same intention is 'blowing out the magic candle'. You do, however, have to believe in magic candles! For some people, this one works more easily than the previous exercise, so let's have a go.

9. THE MAGIC CANDLE

I want you to imagine there is a candle about three feet in front of you. Either sitting or standing, again make sure there is nothing tight around your waist. Without taking a breath, blow out the candle. Push the air out of your lungs and blow out the candle. Of course it's a magic candle and it relights almost immediately. Blow again a little harder. Now remember, there is absolutely no need to 'head butt' the candle. All I've asked you to do is to pump air, from your lungs out through your mouth, using only your tummy muscles. OK?

You may have noticed I didn't tell you to breathe in! If your concentration is on blowing the candle out, not on where you're going to get the air from to do it, your lungs would have refilled by themselves. What I don't want you to do is to take a grab for air before you blow. The effort is only, I repeat only, in blowing the candle out, then letting go.

This is the moment when I usually end up pulling my shirt out of my trousers and showing my tummy! What you're working towards is being able to let your tummy be really relaxed with your lungs full of air, looking as if you were pregnant – with twins. (Yes, I can do that!) And, at will, to be able to push the air out of your lungs by making those muscles rock hard. In fact the moment you think to blow out the candle, the muscles should brace themselves, ready to push the air out. The thought should trigger the muscles. Blow, then let go. Blow, then let go.

Each time you try this exercise see if you can speed the whole process up. Do only a maximum of 10 blows.

Please, don't expect the muscles to instantly come to life. It does take a few days for them to start to understand what you're asking them to do. They will respond, they will get stronger, but probably not today.

MAKING SOUND

Your voice has the potential to make the most wonderful sounds, but only if you're allowing all the muscles to work as they were intended to do. As I've said, these muscles need to be worked gently. Never try and make a lot of sound without warming your voice up properly. This first exercise is the very best way to wake up your voice without doing any damage.

10. HUMMM

Humming is the most wonderful and probably the best way to wake up the sound in your body and is also the basis of how we'll find your 'body note'. Humming wakes up the 'resonators' in your face and in your body. The resonators in your face are like little echo chambers where the sound vibrates. When you are eventually totally 'on voice', humming will clearly show you that the whole of your body is like a sounding board. The sound you're making literally comes through the whole of you. Each of us has a note which is at the core of every sound we make. It is neither sharp or flat, but a whole tone which sets the whole body vibrating, adding harmonics which create a wonderfully complete sound. It's a bit like barbershop singers! The sound is layered, creating the whole. When people say someone has a wonderful voice it's because the sound they are making is coming from the whole of them, not just out of their mouths. As you start to get really on voice you'll feel the sound you're making in your fingertips. It'll be as if you are being given a whole body massage – but from the inside! The sound of your voice will give you an incredible feeling of well-being every time you speak!

1. Sit as before with your bottom in the back of the chair, head floating on a relaxed neck. Put your hand on your tummy and feel the connection with the air you're breathing through your mouth. Relax your jaw. Bring your lips together, allowing your jaw to remain relaxed. Now start to hum very gently. Make sure your tongue is resting on the bottom of your mouth and your throat is relaxed. As you run out of air, open your mouth to let the air back in. Repeat three times.

2. Now try again but this time bring the sound to the front of your lips. To help you think the sound forward, imagine you are moving your lips into the beginning of a kiss and the sound you are making inside your mouth is an 'arh' sound,

not an 'ee'. Keep your tongue resting at the bottom of your mouth. Begin to feel a tingling sensation around your lips. Try three more times.

3. Now try a higher note. Three more times.
4. Now try slowly sweeping up the musical scale.
5. Now try slowly sweeping down.
   Is there a note that, as you pass through it, makes more of you tingle than the others? Hopefully there is.
6. If you've managed to find it, hum three more times on that note.
7. Now try again, but push the air out of your lungs a little harder, almost as if you were trying to blow the candle out but with a hum.
8. Three more times. And rest.

OK, if you've been lucky you will have started to wake up the resonators in your face. The sound box, which is your head, has started to come alive again. Don't worry if it hasn't. Go through the exercises again later, remembering the purpose is to allow the sound to vibrate a little more inside your head. Perhaps you could do the relaxation in the previous chapter before you try this one again. The more relaxed you are, the easier it will be to feel these sensations. However small they are at first, they grow stronger as you get in touch with your state of harmony. Remember, you are rediscovering something that has probably been dormant for years.

11. Hum Arh!

Let's assume you've managed all that. Sit down as before. This time you are going to do the gentle version of the hum you did right at the beginning of this sequence. Do three more until it feels comfortable.

This time, halfway through the hum, open your lips into an 'arh' sound. Make sure its not 'a' as in 'at'. Don't use your jaw or your neck to help, just allow the lips to fall open. Make sure your throat isn't trying to help. This is a very open sound. Three more.

Now imagine you are sending the sound towards the magic candle, so push the air out a little harder. Remember, no head butting! Make sure you're not including your head, neck or throat in any of this. It's crucial you don't start to tighten your throat. If you feel you are, try 'hum arh' with the tip of your tongue between your lips when you start to hum, keeping it with your lower lip when you go into the 'arh'. This will keep the back of your tongue away from the back of your throat.

The effort should only come from the tummy muscles. You can almost see the sound moving out of your mouth in an arc towards the candle. The sound isn't tight in any way, just open and free. It's a connection between your tummy muscles and the magic candle, a connection through sound.

Repeat three more times and rest.

You've now produced, I hope, the beginnings of a clear open sound, one of the many forms of the vowel 'a'. The exercise that follows will include more vowel sounds, but each will start with a consonant. This is when it gets tricky. The temptation is to keep the throat tight when the vowel explodes out of the consonant. You need to remember that open feeling you had with 'arh' and move to it quite rapidly. If you don't, your throat will get in the way. What I don't want is for the back of your throat to play any part in anything you ever say. Remember, wrecked throats wreck speeches!

12. IMPROVING THE AGILITY OF YOUR MOUTH AND STRENGTHENING YOUR DIAPHRAGM!

I want you to make the following sounds in all their detail. Let's take the first line: Mah Nah Mah Nah Mah Nah. When you make the 'M' and 'N' sounds, I want them to be really powered by your tummy muscles, as if you were going to blow the magic candle out. When you open your lips to make the 'arh' sound the air is pushed out by your tummy muscles, like a dam opening, and the sound shoots across the room. The 'N' is the same, except the tip of the tongue is in the roof of your open mouth. The important thing is to start the sounds in your tummy. Over the next few days I want you to start to build in power. However, yet again, please don't overdo it at the beginning. Just be aware that your tummy muscles will get stronger.

Repeat each of the following lines four times before you move on to the next. If you've found the note that makes your face vibrate, use it. If not, pick one a couple of notes lower than your usual speaking voice. Imagine you are a priest intoning all on one note.

Mah Nah Mah Nah Mah Nah
Buh Duh Guh Duh
Wah Bah Dah
Wah Wee Way Woo
Tah Tee Tay Too
Wah Vah Tah Thah

Build in power, so that the vowel explodes out of the consonant. You should feel the effort in your tummy muscles... They **will** and **must** get stronger!

As I hope you're realizing, the magic candle is rather important to what we're now doing. Next time you do this exercise, try making the vowel sound longer and more sustained. Also make sure you work all the detail of the sounds you're making a little more each time you do them. Don't be lazy! Build your muscle power!

13. Speaking While Holding your Nose!

There are a great number of people, who, when they speak, send most of the sound up their nose instead of out of their mouths. Sounds silly, I know, but they do. It's as if they've got a permanent nasal cold. There are even those who think they're making a wonderful sound by doing it. It sounds to them as if their head is full of resonance, although it's actually only their nose that's vibrating. The sounds get locked up inside their nose, giving a very muffled feeling to the words they say. We all do it a bit some of the time. I just want to be sure you're not one of those who does it most of the time!

So, gently squeeze your nostrils with your finger and thumb. If you don't know the poem you are going to read, make sure you can see the page. At last I've got you breathing through your mouth! The only sounds which should go into your nose and then only very briefly are 'M's and 'N's – nothing else!

Say the poem:

Mary had a little lamb,
Its fleece was white as snow,
And everywhere that Mary went,
The lamb was sure to go.

Perhaps you found that when you said the poem the sound stayed in your nose all the time? Or, when you said the words with 'M's and 'N's in them, did the sound stay in your nose a little bit longer than was really necessary?

Try saying the poem again, but this time make the 'M' and 'N' sounds shorter and bring the sound straight back out of your mouth. To help this, imagine you are forming the words about nine inches in front of your mouth.

Clarity of sound improves other people's ability to hear you and builds your confidence, knowing that you are truly being heard. The next exercise I'm going to give you takes this to the most amazing level.

Most people have lazy lips. They barely use them at all to speak. And virtually no one in our tight-lipped society uses their top lip at all! But you need to use your lips to hit the consonants properly. If you don't, the word will not carry. The consonants cut the air, giving the separation to the sounds making up a word. It is possible to be heard at the back of a 3,000-seat theatre without a microphone and without shouting if you hit your consonants. Many actors do it every night!

Now, if you found the last exercise a bit embarrassing, you're going to love this one!

14. SPEAKING WITH YOUR TONGUE OUT!

The exercise I'm going to get you to do does take a little while to get into, as you'll probably spend some minutes on the floor, falling about with hysterics. You will not look a pretty sight, I know, but it does work fantastically well.

Stick your tongue out. Yes that's what I said. Right out! See if you can stop laughing. Relax it! Make sure you don't pull it back in. Yes, I know it's not easy.

Say the poem 'Mary had a little lamb', forming the words only with your lips, without using your tongue. Overwork your lips, especially your top lip, and articulate the words in all their detail. Try it now.

Mary had a little lamb,
Its fleece was white as snow,
And everywhere that Mary went,
The lamb was sure to go.

Well, I reckon you probably made a bit of a mess of that! That's if you were able to speak at all! Yes, I know it feels ridiculous. And yes, you do look stupid.

Now, you probably rushed it and also convinced yourself it was impossible to do. Your tongue may have kept going back into your mouth and probably your lips didn't move at all! Even if you did manage to do some of it, saying 'D's and 'T's with your tongue out may have stopped you in your tracks. Next time, try converting them, with clarity, into 'B's and 'P's. Remember, this is an exercise about getting your lips to work.

It's possible you can't even feel where the muscles are to move your top lip! When you next try it, have a mirror handy to see what is actually going on. Again, don't skip over any of the detail in each word, however difficult it may feel. The muscles will respond a little more each time you try it. Also, to help bring the sound out of your mouth, again imagine your lips are forming the words about nine inches in front of your face. This will help bring your lips forward, just a little, and also help you to remember to push the sound out with your tummy muscles. This exercise is the one I do to wake up my lips. It works every time. The only problem is finding a place to do it that doesn't stop the traffic!

If you've had any success so far, try the poem again with your tongue back inside your mouth and saying it with your newly articulating lips. It should sound very much clearer. Remember, the sound starts with your tummy muscles bracing, then they push the air out of your lungs over your vocal chords, out of your mouth and the words are formed nine inches in front of your mouth.

To fully achieve the open throat you need to allow larger amounts of air both in and out of your lungs, you need a very clear passage for the air to travel along. Most people, when they do breathe through their mouths, unless they are gasping for air, allow very little space for the air to pass through. This is where a great deal of tension is often held. The soft palate is literally held down and the back of the tongue is forced up to meet it. By constricting the airflow in this way, emotions are prevented from getting out.

This next exercise will help to increase the space in the back of your throat.

15. THE SOFT PALATE: NNG GAH

This is tricky to explain. The key to this is the transition from 'N' to 'Gah'. The 'N' sound starts with the tip of your tongue behind your top front teeth. As you move towards the 'G', the tip of the tongue drops down, as the back of the tongue moves up to meet the soft palate. This is the moment in the sound we're exploring. Hold that sound and as you move into the 'Gah', I want you to really open the back of your throat so that the back of your tongue and the soft palate fly apart as the air is forced through.

Repeat this exercise three times only. The soft palate will begin to get stronger and, as it does, the push of the air from your tummy will increase the pressure on it. But as ever, don't be too forceful until you feel confident of what you are doing.

That's it! I've given you the basics on which you can, over a matter of days, feel a significant difference to your vocal quality and power. In a couple of weeks your voice will have a new clarity and strength.

Speaking with increased clarity is the best way of exercising the muscles. But as with everything, the muscles will work best if they are used properly.

On another level, everything we've done so far will give you back the confidence you were born with to make sound. By working with this and the previous section together you will be able to change the pattern of a lifetime. If you can really get to grips with what we've done so far you have the basis of your own emotional and physical warm up and you'll have a far greater success with the next stage of our work together.

Give yourself the time to master what we've done so far before you move on. The more ready your voice is for what's to follow, the more you'll get out of the rest of the book!

Now, the best way to build on this work is to talk.

CHAPTER SEVEN

TALKING THROUGH TEXTS

MOVING YOUR MOUTH

For the whole of this section, if you have a tape recorder or a video camera, I'd ideally like you to be brave enough to use it to record what we're going to be doing, so that you can check for yourself how accurately you're progressing. This is definitely not a cue to start performing! I really only want you to hear and see the changes that take place as you progress. You don't *have* to tape yourself, it's only an option.

This section is not about perfection, it's about feeling the difference. So don't start trying to go for a finished result. And definitely no acting!

Please remember to do your 'Letting Go' and a basic vocal warm up before you start. The voice is a delicate set of muscles that need to be warm before you start working them.

Now, you may be tempted to rush this section. Please don't. Imagine you're learning the moves to a dance or learning to drive a car. It's crucial to take it step by step. If you don't you'll either trip or crash! There'll be aspects you already believe you know and understand. But they need to be experienced in the context of this particular dance. In a short space of time, you'll master what we're doing and very soon it'll become second nature. In fact, it's your original nature which has probably got a bit lost on the way.

Remember, talking is finally all about emotions, not intellect. If you assume you know what you're doing just in your head, rather than feeling it in your guts, it won't work. Put your mask in a safe place while you're working and allow the child inside you to come out and play!

WORDS

What you're going to do now is to start to see and say words as if for the very first time. I want you to explore the sound and detail of each word – one word at a time, breathing between each one. I don't want you to read the words like a list. I want you to feel each word as you say it and after you've said it. Feeling comes with breathing. Only when you've felt a word move on to the next word. Enjoy each word and your ability to bring out its every detail – the consonants, the vowels and the transitions between them, especially the transitions. They're what strengthen your vocal muscles the most. Every single word we use is made up of many sounds. Don't skip over any detail! This is your opportunity to practise your newfound dynamic clarity! If this is a new day, have you done your relaxation and vocal warm up? OK, I want you to sit in the straight-backed chair, bottom in the back of the seat, spine straight, head floating on a relaxed neck and shoulders. Hold the book just below your neckline with your left hand. Put your right hand on your tummy, palm below and thumb above your tummy button.

Start the word in your tummy muscles. Feel them brace, ready to push the air out to form the word about nine inches in front of your mouth. Breathe through your mouth after each and every word. Remember, push the air out with your tummy muscles, then, when you relax them, the air will come back in by itself. Breathe through your mouth!

OK, slowly, one word at a time:

use	their	up	store	labour	of	fruit	gather
remained	same	changed	last	soil	work	always
longing	cut	compared	discontented	joyful	catch
wild	crash	food	trade	cried	treated	wonderful
must	sacrifice	immediately	cut	need	drag	happy
free	except	scratch	ecstatic	dread	hopefully	stop

Just in case you skipped a few of the details, let's look at two of the words you've just said and pull them apart.

'Immediately' is made up of five syllables or parts: *Imm mead ee ate lee*. However, the changes the mouth has to make to create the sounds from the I to M, M to E, E to D, D to E, E to A, A to T, T to L, and L to E form eight transitions in all, each of which, if not clear, can confuse the ear of the listener.

This is just one word. You could easily say, 'But people understand what I'm saying.' Well, yes, that's probably true, most of the time, when they're close to you and know your voice. If you aren't clear, they'll try to help themselves understand what you're saying by reading your lips and face. But what if they're 50 feet away? Remember also, if you're nervous, the mouth starts to lock up and even 'immediately' could become unintelligible. Try saying 'unintelligible' quickly! I'm preparing you for when you are under great pressure. Your usual vocal ability just won't do. The other aspect I want you to experience is the effect the word has on you, as you say it. Every word carries with it its own power, handed on from generation to generation. It also has a very specific emotional effect on your organized energy system!

Let's take the word 'scratch'. What does the sound of the word make you feel? Does it tense you up or is there a strange release of a feeling that's been held inside?

Maybe you hear 'scratch' as a noun. When did you last have a scratch? What did it feel like? Was it large? Did you have a bandage on it? How did you get it? Maybe you hear it as a verb. Did you scratch your car? Did you scratch your leg because you had an itch? Have you ever scratched your eye? There's a multitude of possibilities, all held within that one word made up of five vocal transitions. Amazing!

> Say the words again and start to experience them as well as articulating them.

'Ah'

Something I haven't really touched on yet is the ending of words. Finishing words is something which adds great strength to anything you say, but not many people do it!

I've discovered that when I want to add that extra edge to the end of the word or when I need to carry it over longer distances or I want to be more forceful, I imagine each word has an 'ah' on the end of it. So 'cut' becomes 'cutah', 'breathe' becomes 'breatheah', and so on.

> Say each of the words in the list again and after you've said it in all its detail, including the 'ah' on the end, breathe. Try it now.
>
> This is your chance to practise pumping a lot of air into each word. Use it up, let go, allow the air to come back in to your lungs as you feel the word you have just said.

OK, did the words come alive a little more, both physically and emotionally? Hopefully you started to really feel each word a little more as you said it. Words are so powerful in their own right. If you say them well and clearly they'll give you the energy for what you want to say next. Really!

FABLES

Next, I'm going to ask you to say an Aesop's fable. 'Say', not 'read'! First, I'd like you to say it one word at a time. The temptation will be either to scan ahead of the word you're saying or to read it like a list. Please don't. Also, don't read the whole story before you say it and don't even think about 'acting' or performing. Just let the words speak for themselves. Experience each word. Use a lot of air on each word (remember the magic candle) and add a slight 'ah' sound to the end to give it clarity.

A shepherd boy was sitting tending his flock near his village. He decided it would be great fun to hoax the villagers by pretending a wolf was attacking the sheep. So he got up and ran towards the village shouting, 'Wolf! Wolf!' When the people of the village came rushing to his aid, he laughed at them for their efforts. He did this again and again, and every time the villagers came to his aid, but every time they found they had been hoodwinked. There was no wolf.

One day a wolf really did come and the boy rushed towards the village and cried, 'Wolf! Wolf!' as loudly as he could. The people of the village were so used to hearing him call out that they decided to take no notice of his cries for help. So the wolf had it all his own way and killed all the sheep at his leisure.

You cannot believe a liar even when he tells the truth.

Have a rest, you've been pumping a lot of air. When you've recovered, I want you to try something very special. I want you to say the story again, but this time I want you to see each thought, each picture you are presented with. Let's look at the first sentence:

A shepherd boy was sitting tending his flock near his village.

The first image you have is 'a shepherd boy'. Say only that and breathe, but don't move on. As you breathe, picture the boy. Place him in front of you in the room. See him.

'Was sitting' is the next thought. Stay with that as you breathe and see the little boy sitting down in the room.

Next is 'tending'. Breathe. What was he tending? Probably the sheep, although could it be his knee that he's scratched? I wonder.

The next thought is 'his flock'. Breathe. I thought so, I knew it was the sheep. See them around him.

The next thought is 'near'. Breathe. Near what? A lake?

The next thought is 'his village'. Breathe. Ah, his village. Of course. Imagine the village is just outside the room you're sitting in.

OK? Try it now.

What you've just done, very slowly, is to go through what you do incredibly quickly when you have the perfect conversation. As I hope you remember, in a perfect conversation, whether you're the speaker or the listener, you engage in an exchange of images, thoughts and emotions. You don't think in sentences, but say, one thought at a time, what's in your mind. The listener repeats it under their breath and then you listen, with them, to what you've just said. That's when you breathe, together, while you also check whether they've understood. They'll probably nod involuntarily if they're with you. And magically the next thought will be there in your mind ready to be spoken. You both experience what you've said at the same moment. You're connected by the thought. You see, even when one person is doing all the talking, ideally, it's still a two-way conversation. The listener is part of the process.

Say the fable again, but this time I want you to imagine you're telling this story to a young child. There's no rush to tell it. The idea is for the child to enjoy each element, each thought. Give them time to paint their picture. If you rush it, the child has to try and remember what you've just said and break it back down into thoughts and pictures. While they do this they'll miss what you say next. And then, I'm afraid to say, you've lost them!

Say the story to the child, remembering to articulate each word with energy, in all its detail. Stay with the word and the thought – don't scan ahead. Breathe between each and every thought. Breathe with the child. Make sure they've got each picture before you move on. There is no hurry! Listen to what you are saying very carefully. Give yourself and the child time to enjoy the story as it unfolds. Don't be tempted to act it. Let the words tell the story to both of you.

I want you to breathe after every comma and full stop, after every single thought. You may want to say to me, 'But we don't breathe after every single thought!' I know, but these are exercises to explore something you haven't done since you first learned to talk. Try and put your brain in neutral and begin again to breathe and feel! Say the story now.

A shepherd boy, was sitting, tending, his flock, near,
his village. He decided, it would be, great fun, to hoax,
the villagers, by pretending, a wolf, was attacking, the sheep.
So he got up, and ran, towards the village, shouting,
'Wolf! Wolf!' When the people, of the village, came rushing,
to his aid, he laughed at them, for their efforts. He did this,
again and again, and every time, the villagers, came, to his aid,
but every time, they found, they had been, hoodwinked.
There was, no wolf. One day, a wolf, really did come,
and the boy, rushed, towards the village, and cried,
'Wolf! Wolf!' as loudly, as he could. The people, of the village,
were so used, to hearing him, call out, that they decided,

to take, no notice, of his cries, for help. And so, the wolf,
had it all, his own way, and killed, all the sheep, at his leisure.
You cannot, believe, a liar, even when, he tells, the truth.

OK, you may well have got in a muddle with all these changes I've
asked for, but if you've been lucky, some moments in the story will
have really come alive. Did you say 'Wolf! Wolf!' with a bit more
power and energy in your voice? Did you pump a bit of air?

What you've just tried to do is the essence of everything we're going
to do together. You've re-created the basic elements of the perfect
conversation, and, I can't say it often enough, talking to people, however many, is always a conversation.

Let's try another fable. This time let's imagine you are a rather cyn-
ical journalist and a story is coming in on the wire. You don't know
what it's about and you comment after each thought. Add any
comment you like, as long as it relates to what's just been said! I'll
give you a taster of what I mean:

There was (what?) a time (oh great! a heavy opener!) when
the frogs (a story about frogs?! Do we really need this!)
became discontented (I know the feeling, this is rubbish)
because they had no one (so what!) to rule over them. (Ah,
now we're getting there, it's a monarchy story!) So they sent
(yes, yes!) a deputation (this sounds big) to Jupiter (wow,
frogs and gods!) to ask (ask what, ask what?!) if he would
give them (I know, I know) a king. (Got it, 'Sexist frogs beg
gods for male monarch!')

Get the idea? React to what you read!

There was, a time, when the frogs, became discontented,
because, they had, no one, to rule over them. So they sent,
a deputation, to Jupiter, to ask, if he would give them,
a king. Jupiter, seeing, their request, as foolish, cast, a log,
into the pond, where they lived, and told them, the log,
was to be, their new king. The frogs, were so terrified,
by the log, as it hit, the water, they scurried away,
into the deepest parts, of the pond. Gradually, as they saw,
the log, didn't move, one by one, they came back,
up to the surface again. Before long, as they grew, bolder,
they started, to feel, so contemptuous, towards the log,
that they even took, to sitting on it. Believing, a king,
of that sort, was, an insult, to their dignity, they sent,
a deputation, to Jupiter, for a second time. They begged him,
to take away, the sluggish king, he had given them.
They asked, to be given, another, and better, king.
Annoyed, at being pestered, in this way, Jupiter, sent, a stork,
to rule, over them. No sooner, had the stork, arrived,
among them, than she began, to catch, and eat, the frogs,
as quickly, as she possibly could.

Now say it again a little quicker (that does not mean fast), either as
the journalist or to the child, who's still sitting there. Ideally do it
both ways.

Even though you are speeding up, I still want you to breathe
between each and every thought. Don't just pause. If you are pushing the air out with your tummy braced and then letting go, enough
air will come back into your lungs. You will be replenished.

It will sound a bit as though you're blowing out the candle. But
that's what I want for now. Remember, everything we're doing is
an exercise and the more you absorb what's happening at this stage,
the easier the rest will be. Don't take the words for granted. Just let
them tell the story. And, as I've already said, don't start acting!

Verbs

Let's go back to the first story. Say it again to the child, only this time, I want you to make the verbs, the words which tell us what's happening, longer. Over-explain them, as if the child had never heard these words before.

A shepherd boy, was **sitting, tending,** his flock,
near his village. He **decided,** it would **be,** great fun, to **hoax,**
the villagers, by **pretending,** a wolf, was **attacking,**
the sheep. So he **got up,** and **ran,** towards the village,
shouting, 'Wolf! Wolf!' When the people, of the village,
came rushing, to his aid, he **laughed** at them,
for their efforts. He **did** this, again and again, and every time,
the villagers, **came,** to his aid, but every time, they **found,**
they **had been hoodwinked.** There **was,** no wolf. One day,
a wolf, really **did come,** and the boy, **rushed,**
towards the village, and **cried,** 'Wolf! Wolf!' as loud,
as he **could.** The people, of the village, were so **used,**
to **hearing** him, **call out,** that they **decided,** to **take,** no notice,
of his cries for help. And so, the wolf, **had** it all, his own way,
and **killed,** all the sheep, at his leisure. You cannot, **believe,**
a liar, even when he **tells,** the truth.

The purpose of extending the verbs is that they're the actions of the story. They tell us what's happening. They move the story on. They're the energy and life of the story. They're the emotion and stories are all about emotion! Many people will emphasize every other possible word except the verbs because they're trying to put some feeling into what they're saying, but they end up putting a generalized wash of emotion onto words like 'and' and 'but' and 'with', which becomes totally meaningless!

Verbs Plus Nouns

When we first learn to read we're taught that the key parts of what we say are the noun and the verb. When we're speaking to someone, we actually check with them if they heard them. This is another element of the perfect conversation. The nouns tell the listener who and what you're talking about while the verbs tell them what's happening.

What you're now going to say is a story which is full of facts made up of verbs and nouns, a 'news story'. Don't fall into the trap that many people make of sounding like a bad newsreader. Many speakers end up emphasizing every fourth word, whatever it is, by dropping its pitch. We don't drop the pitch like that in real life, unless we're clinically depressed! This strange, fixed sing-song of sound tells you the speaker is not really listening to what they're saying.

To help you to achieve the perfect conversation, imagine this time you're explaining this story to a 13-year-old girl who is very bright, but not worldly. She is still learning about the world and you don't want her to misunderstand anything you're saying. This means you don't assume anything. You check that she's understood each and every thought. Give her time to work out where you are in the world, who you are talking about and what exactly is happening. Don't talk down to her, remember she's bright. The advantage you have the first time through this story is you don't know the story either! You'll learn what is going on together.

Remember, don't read ahead of what you are actually saying! Also, continue to breathe between each thought.

Aboard Air Force One, President Bush, signed, the Aid Bill,
on his way, to South Carolina. Arriving, at dawn,
he was to see, one of the worst hit states. But even though,
the debris, was being cleared, it's the human problems,
authorities, must now face. In this state alone, 60,000,
are homeless, half a million, displaced, and almost 300,000,

out of work. President Bush, was using, this first visit,
to the disaster front line, to answer, his critics, who say,
the US government, has done, too little,
for the storm's victims. From Charleston, he was driven,
along a route, littered, with trees, snapped in half,
and house after house, showing, the scars, left, by Hugo.
In Summerville, he saw, a community, battling, to overcome,
the difficulties, caused, by the hurricane. President Bush,
answered, his critics, by saying, that once the debris,
was cleared, people, would realize, there had been,
a total team effort. Part of the money, in the hurricane fund,
already approved, by Congress, will go, to retrain,
displaced workers, and provide, continued,
emergency services.

With luck much of what you've just done started to sound as though it wasn't a text you were reading. Did you also remember to articulate all the words, in all their detail? Did you put an 'ah' on the end of words? Did you sustain the pitch at the end of each thought? Did you breathe through your mouth between each thought?

I'm sure you did everything perfectly. But just in case you didn't, I've re-written the news report with pretty well everything marked that can be marked! The nouns are in italic and the verbs are in bold. Put the nouns almost in inverted commas. They're what you're talking about. We need time to take them in. The verbs need to be made longer, as before, to fill them with energy. They tell us what's happening to the nouns and allow us to feel.

OK, try this version:

Aboard, *Air Force One, President Bush,* **signed,** the *Aid Bill,*
on his way, to *South Carolina.* **Arriving,** at *dawn,*
he **was to see,** one of the *worst hit states.*

But even though the *debris*, **was being cleared,**
it's the *human problems*, *authorities*, **must now face.**
In this *state* alone, *60,000*, **are homeless,** *half a million,*
displaced, and almost *300,000*, **out of work.** *President Bush,*
was using, this *first visit*, to the *disaster front line*, to **answer,**
his *critics*, who **say,** the *US government*, **has done,** too *little,*
for the *storm's victims.* From *Charleston*, he **was driven,**
along a *route*, **littered,** with *trees,* **snapped** in half,
and *house* after *house*, **showing,** the *scars,* **left** by *Hugo.*
In *Summerville*, he **saw,** a *community*, **battling,** to **overcome,**
the *difficulties*, **caused,** by the *hurricane.* *President Bush,*
answered, his *critics*, by **saying,** that once the *debris,*
was cleared, *people*, **would realize,** there **had been,**
a *total team effort.* **Part** of the *money*, in the *hurricane fund,*
already **approved,** by *Congress*, **will go,** to retrain,
displaced workers, and **provide,** *continued,*
emergency services.

What I've reproduced is a written version of the basic conversation pattern, along with everything else you've done. You may well feel it bears very little resemblance to anything you've yet said to another human being! But I assure you, these are the steps of the dance you do whenever you're with someone with whom you're totally relaxed. You've just never broken it down like this before. No, that's not true. The last time you did was when you were very, very young!

You need to be certain you've got your breathing and your lips moving. So don't neglect the mouth and breathing exercises. Once you feel confident that your 'equipment' is working well, use any or all of the texts here to explore your ability to recreate a conversation. What I've given you is the structure and the tools to turn something you're reading into something that can really come alive when you speak it.

You'll soon begin to feel you are really communicating more fully both your thoughts and feelings when you get up and talk.

What we'll do next is to develop further your ability to really communicate emotion. Don't worry, this doesn't mean you're going to have to cry, not unless you want to!

As I've said before, don't rush on to the next section. It's much better for you to be really comfortable with what we've done so far. I know that for many people the desire to 'just do it' is always there, perhaps because they don't want to look too deeply at what's going on inside them. But I hope by now you realize that that really isn't anything to be afraid of.

PETER PIPER

Just for fun, see if your mouth can get round this tongue twister, in all its detail! Breathe between each word, with your hand on your tummy. Magic candle, magic candle, magic candle! OK, *go!*

Peter, Piper, picked, a, peck, of, pickled, pepper.
If, Peter, Piper, picked, a, peck, of, pickled, pepper,
Where's, the peck, of, pickled, pepper, Peter, Piper, picked?

MY NAME IS...

Finally, I want you to stand in front of a mirror and say the full name you were given at birth in all its glorious detail. Say, 'My name is...' and breathe between each word.

When I ask people to do this, they often find it really hard at first. These few words that make up your name have so much emotional energy contained within them, it's almost shocking. Your past passes before you as you say them. How you say them will tell you a lot about how you're feeling about yourself. See whether you can

---

say your name without looking away, without commenting and without making any judgement on yourself whatsoever.

EXPLORING THE POWER OF TEXTS

In this section you're going to explore some texts from plays. But NO ACTING! You're going to take further what you've already started to do – allow the words to touch you. But the words, not you, will tell the story. So often we impose something on a text from our head, never giving our heart time to be heard. Talking from the heart is another way of saying 'allowing your child to have their voice'. If you allow your child to speak, as we have seen, you'll find something more truthful and honest will emerge, something that your listeners will truly hear.

The speeches we're going to be using are from various plays. Some were written for women and some for men, but all of them were written to be spoken. I want you to work through them all, whatever your gender!

Again, please don't rush through this section. As before, give yourself time to really experience each stage before you move on.

UNCLE VANYA

When you begin this speech you'll find I've marked the text. At each comma, full stop, and dash, I want you to breathe. If you want, you can have even more breaths. There is no hurry. Don't read ahead. I want you to stay with each thought and let it sink into you before you move on. Let yourself really experience the words you're saying. Let them paint their vivid picture in your mind's eye. Let yourself feel what it's like to be the person who's speaking.

Sit in the straight-backed chair, bottom in the back of the seat, spine straight, head floating on relaxed neck and shoulders, holding the book just below your neckline with your left hand. Put your right hand on your tummy, palm below and thumb above your tummy button. Start the word in your tummy muscles. Feel them brace, ready to push the air out to form the word, about nine inches in front of your mouth. Breathe after each and every thought (after each and every comma and full stop). Remember, push the air out with your tummy muscles, then, when you relax them, the air will come back in, all by itself – through your mouth!

OK, slowly, one thought at a time, remembering this is an exercise not a performance, very gently:

There's nothing worse, than knowing, someone's secret,
and not being able, to help. He's not, in love with her,
that's obvious – but why shouldn't he, marry her?
She's not pretty, but she'd make, an excellent wife,
for a country doctor, at his time of life. She's intelligent,
and so kind and pure... No, that's not the point...
I understand, the poor girl, so well. In the middle of all this,
desperate boredom, with just grey shadows,
wandering around, instead of human beings,
with nothing, but common-place tittle-tattle, to listen to,
from people, who do nothing, but eat, drink, and sleep,
he appears, from time to time – so different,
from the rest of them. Handsome, interesting, attractive,
like a bright moon, arising, in the darkness ... to fall,
under the fascination, of a man like that, to forget one-self...
I believe, I'm a little attracted myself... Yes, I'm bored,
when he's not about, and here I am, smiling,
when I think of him... Uncle Vanya here, says, I have,
mermaid's blood, in my veins. 'Let yourself go,
for once in your life.' Well, perhaps that's what I ought,
to do... To fly away, free as a bird, away from all of you,
from your sleepy faces, and talk, to forget,
that you exist at all – everyone of you! But I'm,
too timid and shy... My conscience, would torment me,
to distraction... He comes here, every day... I can guess,

why he comes, and already, I feel guilty... I want to fall,
on my knees, before Sonia, to ask, her forgiveness, and cry.

The text you've just said is from the play *Uncle Vanya* by the Russian writer Anton Chekhov. It was written in 1900. Yeliena is a beautiful, intelligent young woman. She is the second wife of a retired professor. Sonia, her stepdaughter, has just admitted to her that she's in love with Astrov, a doctor. In this speech, Yeliena reveals how bored she is with country life and discovers that she is half in love with Astrov herself.

But then you knew a lot of that already, didn't you, if you were listening to what you were saying? I hope you gave yourself the time and space to breathe and feel each thought, and by listening and experiencing what you were saying, allowed the story to speak to you.

I'd like you to say it again, just as you did before and re-experience what you felt, by letting the words in, all over again.

There's always the temptation to try and copy what you've done before, by-passing your emotions. But the more you can allow yourself to connect to your true emotions, the easier it will be to repeat something you have said before and for it to become real, every single time, for you and for the listener. Try it again now.

I hope you were able to re-experience the speech afresh. Also, as the words became more familiar, you probably felt easier about letting your feelings just happen.

This time I want you to imagine a very dear friend is sitting in the room with you. Someone you can take all the time in the world to tell the story to. There's no hurry. You know they'll wait. Take your eyes off the page and give them each and every thought, allowing time for you both to breathe and react, before you look down and move on to the next thought.

I hope by now you are able to feel the beginnings of how, if you stay in the moment of what you're saying, you don't have to do anything with the words. You don't have to 'perform' them.

If you're happy with how you did, let's do it again, but this time standing up. Sound the trumpets! You're going to start to use a little more energy.

Still breathe at all the commas, full stops and dashes, but this time imagine your friend has moved to the other side of the room.

The first thing that's likely to happen is your voice will go higher and you'll shout. Don't! Keep the note coming from your tummy muscles, not from your throat. Use all the air up on each thought and then let go. You can breathe more than once after each thought, but don't grab for air. Try to look at your friend when you're talking to them, imagine them responding and remember to breathe.

OK, legs apart, knees slightly bent, head floating on relaxed neck and shoulders, book at chest height. Feel your space and don't lean forward to try and reach the other person. Feel your child in your tummy and speak from there.

You've now done your first piece of text standing up, bravo! How did it feel? Did you start to act? Did you start to squeak? Did you start to lean forwards? Did you lean backwards or did you hold your ground? Did you see your listener there? Did they listen? Did you listen? Did you breathe? Repeat this exercise until you really feel happy that you've found a level which is real, not fake.

Say goodbye to your friend for now. This time, I'd like you to imagine there's someone in the room who's deliberately not understanding what you're saying. So you have to explain it very clearly to them, articulating each word very carefully – very emphatically with energy. Emphasize the verbs as you did in previous texts by making them longer and stronger to make sure the person understands. Make them listen by being firm and clear about what you're saying, not by leaning in and shouting. Lastly, don't act, don't perform. I know it sounds as if I'm asking you to, but let the words speak for themselves. Concentrate on being understood by someone who doesn't want to listen. The emotion will, I assure you, take care of itself.

OK, in your own time.

Did you hold the person's attention? Did you get irritated that they weren't listening to you? Did they remind you of someone in your life? A lover, a parent, your boss?

Try it one more time and put someone you know out there. Really picture them, really feel what it's like when you try and talk to them and they don't listen to you properly. Make sure you don't start pleading with them or whining. Put your hand on your tummy and push air!

OK, I hope you began to experience how a text, which you'd assume has nothing to do with you, can reach into some aspects of your own life.

Now, I'd like you to hand it over completely to the child in you. You may already feel you've done this, but I'd like you to quietly go back and sit down and very softly let the child say it all by themselves, to you. Put your hand on your tummy and allow them to speak from there. Very relaxed, very open, very easy, very gently ... begin.

Epitaph for George Dillon

This next speech is from a play by John Osborne called *Epitaph for George Dillon*.

I'd like you to say it just as you did the first time through with the previous speech, saying each word clearly and gently. Breathe between each thought and allow it to touch you before you move on to the next one. I have marked the text for you. Allow the character who is talking to connect to you as the words come out of your mouth. Picture what you're saying and allow yourself to feel what you're saying. Don't scan ahead and don't pre-read the speech.

The one thing, I never shoot, lines about, is the R.A.F.
Just a gap, in my life. That's all. Well, it happened, like this:
It was, one night, in particular, when it wasn't, my turn, to go,
on ops. Instead, we got, a basinful, of what we gave,
the Jerries, smack bang, in the middle, of the camp.
I remember, flinging myself down, not so much,
on to the earth, as into it. A Wing Commander type,
pitched himself, next to me, and together, we shared,
his tin-helmet. Fear, ran through, the whole, of my body,
the strange fear, that my right leg, would be blown off,
and how terrible, it would be. Suddenly, the winco,
shouted at me, above the din, 'What's your profession?'
'Actor,' I said. The moment, I uttered, that word,
machine-gun fire, and bombs, all around us,
the name of my calling, my whole reason,
for existence – it sounded, so hideously trivial,

and unimportant, so divorced, from living, and the real world,
that my fear, vanished. All I could feel, was shame.
(He is lost for a moment or two. Then he adds brightly)
Gifted people, are always, dramatizing themselves.
It provides, its own experience, I suppose.

I hope you started to feel you were actually there. Really imagined
and felt the story you were telling.

OK, this time, like the previous speech, say it as if you're talking to
a very dear friend – very relaxed, very easy, but with gentle clarity.
Breathe with them, as you both hear and see and feel what you've
just said. See and feel your friend reacting as you tell the story, as
the words tell their story.

Now I'd like you to say it to the very young child you told the fable
to. Try not to talk to them in a childish way as if they're stupid,
more as if you want to paint the pictures very vividly. I'd like you
to get up and move around the room and really make the story happen for them! See each part of the story happening there and then.
Be in the thought. Remember to get down when the bombs drop
and have the 'winco' next to you when you're talking to him. If you
lose your place in the text, keep breathing – through your mouth!

Hopefully you didn't damage yourself! That was a rather more physical version of what we all do when we get a bit carried away with our
stories. If you were very half-hearted about doing it that way, I want
you to have another go! Be brave and dramatic and relive the story.

This time I'd like you to bring back the 13-year-old girl you spoke
to before into your room – remember she's very intelligent, but not
worldly. Treat her like a very young adult and explain carefully each

stage of the story. Enjoy explaining each detail to her. Instead of doing what you did with the small child, I want you to stay seated and use one of your hands to show her what's happening. If you dived under the table when the bombs started falling before, point to the table and see yourself there all over again. Be there in your mind's eye. Live the story from the safety of your chair!

I'd like you to now say it to the young girl as if you were a very pompous old man with a very plummy voice – someone who goes 'errm' a lot and forgets what he's talking about, so there are long pauses. So there's no hurry! This doesn't mean I want you to act the words. Sit down and just imagine being ancient and tired. Start to breathe as if you were that age. Make a few 'errm' sounds as you breathe out. Imagine you've had a couple of drinks. Now start the speech, but let the words do everything else, not you.

How was that? Was it very tempting to act it? Hopefully you found that the words came out differently just by breathing, by feeling different. Acting is imagining a different part of you and saying the words, not saying the words 'differently'. If you're listening, the words will do it for you all by themselves!

Finally I'd like you to do as before and just let your child say the speech in all their simplicity. Let the words come from them.

This is where I want you to start making choices for yourself. What you've done so far is to give the words time to speak to you, to breathe each single thought at the commas and full stops and experience it fully before you moved on. On a practical level this helped you to get your lungs really working and build up their strength – magic candle, magic candle! – and also to break down the patterns every person goes into when they first try to read out loud. They end up faking what they're feeling, because they're not really listening to what they're saying, they're presenting it. There are no real thoughts and images, no real feelings. The words don't touch them. Nor do they touch the person who's listening. There is no conversation!

If you ever get up to talk to anyone, you need to have a very powerful belief you can breathe and feel between each and every thought any time you need to, just like you do in the perfect conversation. You must now decide how often you want to breathe, but please continue to break what you're saying into thoughts, which means there's still a beat pause between each and every one. The temptation will be to try and speak for as long as you can without taking a breath, or at least skip over the thoughts and just get and give a general feel of what you're saying. But if you do that you'll lose everything we're trying to achieve. Please don't cut off from *feeling* what you're saying.

GUILT AND GINGERBREAD

This next speech is from a play by Lionel Hale called *Guilt and Gingerbread*.

Again, I'd like you to say this speech thought by thought, but this time there are no extra markings. If you're truly listening to what you're saying, you'll break the speech up naturally into thoughts. Imagine the story is being fed to you thought by thought. The nouns and the verbs will tell you when to pause and breathe. This first time through, say it quietly to yourself but out loud, still with clarity, very slowly, thought by thought.

I call it a damned outrage. I am lunching perfectly quietly at the Ritz with a woman friend, and every time I try to look out at St James's Park, there you are sitting at a table in the window by yourself, staring at me. You. A perfect stranger,

staring. And you are still staring. I go off alone to the Curzon
Cinema to see a film about two dwarfs making love in a cellar,
in French: and I get bored with it, naturally enough, after half
an hour, and I come out: and who seems to have got bored
with it at the same moment and comes out too? You do. You.
I get into my car and am driven to South Molton Street to buy
a hat. That hat. It's probably a perfectly dreadful hat, because
I'm still upset about those two French dwarfs in a cellar. And I
step into my car, and there you are halfway down South
Molton Street, getting yourself a taxi. And when I arrive
home, and let myself into my own front door, who calmly follows me in across my own hall and up my own stairs and into
my own drawing room? And there you stand! I have never
been so insulted in my life. I don't know you from Adam; but
your behaviour is absolutely intolerable. It's unspeakable. It's
entirely and utterly blackguardly *[blagardly]*. Well, don't go! I
mean to say only that it seems the very worst of manners to go
away without apologizing. I mean to say: it seems pretty cool
to me – nobody asked you to sit down – well, haven't you anything to say?

As you might have heard, she's pretty annoyed, to say the least! How
did you find saying and hearing each thought? Did you find yourself
running on or did you allow yourself time to picture each image and
feel each thought?

I've included my version (opposite), so that you can compare any
differences. My markings, as I've said, break a speech down into its
individual thoughts. In the main, you'll find there is a mark before and
after each noun and before and after each verb.

See if you can start working without the markings, but if you find
you run the thoughts into each other and lose the sense of what you're
saying, go to the marked version. It is so important that you learn to
break a text down into thoughts yourself, for it's a skill which will

make all the difference when you get up to give a speech, even when you're only working with notes! You will be creating much more vivid pictures for both yourself and the audience by really listening and experiencing your thoughts!

MARKED VERSION

I call it, a damned outrage. I am lunching, perfectly quietly,
at the Ritz, with a woman friend, and every time,
I try to look out, at St James's Park, there you are, sitting,
at a table, in the window, by yourself, staring at me. You.
A perfect stranger, staring. And you are still staring.
I go off alone, to the Curzon Cinema, to see a film,
about two dwarfs, making love, in a cellar, in French:
and I get bored with it, naturally enough, after half an hour,
and I come out: and who seems, to have got bored with it,
at the same moment, and comes out too? You do. You.
I get into, my car, and am driven, to South Molton Street,
to buy, a hat. That hat. It's probably, a perfectly dreadful hat,
because I'm still upset, about those two French dwarfs,
in a cellar. And I step into, my car, and there you are,
half way down South Molton Street, getting yourself, a taxi.
And when I arrive, home, and let myself into,
my own front door, who calmly follows me, in across,
my own hall, and up, my own stairs, and into,
my own drawing room? And there, you stand!
I have never been, so insulted, in my life. I don't know you,
from Adam; but your behaviour, is absolutely intolerable.
It's unspeakable. It's entirely, and utterly, blackguardly.
Well, don't go! I mean, to say only, that it seems,
the very worst of manners, to go away, without apologizing.
I mean to say: it seems, pretty cool, to me – nobody,
asked you, to sit down – well, haven't you, anything, to say?

It will be very tempting to act up with this one, but try not to. Not just yet!

OK, before you say it again I want you to remember how you feel when you're irritated and slightly bad-tempered. Move around the room and breathe into that feeling. Feel your breathing change, feel how you move differently how you have a different rhythm. Now bring someone into the room, in your mind's eye. Breathe the feeling of what it's like to be irritated by them. Express the energy you're feeling into the opening words. Don't act angry with the other person. Keep the verbs long and strong. Then let the words do all the work!

With any luck the words did the work for you. As you heard yourself say the first few in a different tone and rhythm, you were fed the feeling that they expressed. Also, by hearing what you said you created your own 'emotional domino effect': the way each thought was expressed affected the way you said the next one. You don't have to manufacture the feeling: that would be 'bad acting'.

Try it again and make sure you're listening to what you're saying and feeling the thoughts before you move on.

This time I'd like you to feel very naughty and wicked with a twinkle in your eye! Allow your child to help you! Imagine someone you've flirted with in the past. Imagine how you felt. Breathe into that feeling. You'll find that flirting and being the child is closer than you think. Move around the room and allow that feeling to flow through you as you begin to speak the first few words to the person on the other side of the room. Then let the words carry you forward with the feelings they give you.

Isn't it amazing how the same set of words can sound so different depending on how you feel?

> Finally sit down and let your child say the speech very gently to you.

LOOK BACK IN ANGER

As this is the last speech from a play you'll be doing, I've deliberately picked a difficult one. Who said it was all going to be easy?! You need to go through it very carefully, thought by thought. Remember the best way to do it is by not scanning ahead, but by saying each thought out loud and, like building blocks, adding one on top of the other. The words are wicked and cruel but also funny. Again, my marked version will follow. Try to work without it, but use it if you feel you are losing the sense of what you're saying.

Say it now, thought by thought, articulating each word so that you really feel the sounds and feelings in the words.

UNMARKED VERSION

The funny thing is, you know, I really did have to ride up on a white charger – off-white, really. Mummy locked her up in their eight-bedroomed castle, didn't she? There is no limit to what the middle-class mummy will do in the holy crusade against ruffians like me. Mummy and I took one quick look at each other, and, from then on, the age of chivalry was dead. I knew that, to protect her innocent young, she wouldn't hesitate to cheat, lie, bully and blackmail. Threatened with me, a young man without money, background or even looks, she'd bellow like a rhinoceros in labour – enough to make every

male rhino for miles turn white, and pledge himself to
celibacy. But even I underestimated her strength. Mummy
may look over-fed and a bit flabby on the outside, but don't let
that well-bred guzzler fool you. Underneath all that, she's
armour-plated – she's as rough as a night in a Bombay
brothel, and as tough as a matelot's arm. She's probably in
that bloody cistern, taking down every word we say. *(Kicks
cistern.)* Can you 'ear me, mother? *(Sits on it, beats like bongo
drums.)* Just about get her in there. Let me give you an example of this lady's tactics. You may have noticed that I happen
to wear my hair rather long. Now, if my wife is honest, or concerned enough to explain, she could tell you that this is not
due to any dark, unnatural instincts I possess, but because *(a)* I
can usually think of better things than a haircut to spend two
bob on, and *(b)* I prefer long hair. But obvious, innocent
explanation didn't appeal to Mummy at all. So she hires
detectives to watch me, to see if she can't somehow get me into
the *News of the World*. All so that I shan't carry off her
daughter on that poor old charger of mine, all tricked out and
caparisoned in discredited passions and ideals! The old grey
mare that actually once led the charge against the old order –
well, she certainly ain't what she used to be. It was all she
could do to carry me, but your weight was too much for her.
She just dropped dead on the way.

Two words which always get people, when they say them:

'matelot', pronounced *mat-low*, which means sailor
'caparisoned', pronounced *cap-aar-is-ond*, which means a
horse's trappings or equipment

MARKED VERSION

The funny thing is, you know, I really did, have to ride up,
on a white charger – off-white, really. Mummy, locked her up,
in their eight-bedroomed castle, didn't she? There is, no limit,
to what the middle-class mummy, will do, in the holy crusade,
against, ruffians like me. Mummy and I, took, one quick look,
at each other, and from then on, the age of chivalry, was dead.
I knew, that to protect, her innocent young,
she wouldn't hesitate, to cheat, lie, bully,
and blackmail. Threatened, with me, a young man,
without money, background, or even looks, she'd bellow,
like a rhinoceros, in labour – enough to make,
every male rhino, for miles, turn white, and pledge himself,
to celibacy. But even I, underestimated, her strength. Mummy,
may look, over-fed, and a bit flabby, on the outside,
but don't let, that well-bred guzzler, fool you.
Underneath all that, she's armour-plated – she's as rough,
as a night, in a Bombay brothel, and as tough,
as a matelot's arm. She's probably, in that bloody cistern,
taking down, every word, we say. *(Kicks cistern.)*
Can you 'ear me, mother? *(Sits on it, beats like bongo drums.)*
Just about get her in there. Let me give you, an example,
of this lady's tactics. You may have noticed,
that I happen, to wear, my hair, rather long. Now, if my wife,
is honest, or concerned enough, to explain, she could tell you,
that this is not due, to any dark, unnatural instincts, I possess,
but because (*a*), I can usually think,
of better things than a haircut, to spend two bob on, and (*b*),
I prefer, long hair. But obviously, innocent explanation,
didn't appeal, to Mummy, at all. So she hires, detectives,
to watch me, to see, if she can't somehow, get me,
into the *News of the World*. All so that I shan't carry off,
her daughter, on that poor old charger of mine, all tricked out,

and caparisoned, in discredited passions, and ideals!
The old grey mare, that actually once led, the charge,
against the old order – well, she certainly ain't,
what she used to be. It was all she could do, to carry me,
but your weight, was too much for her. She just dropped dead,
on the way.

This speech is from another John Osborne play called *Look Back in Anger*. As the title suggests, the character Jimmy is a little irritated with his mother-in-law. He is talking to his best friend, with his own wife in the room as well.

> When you feel you are comfortable with the thoughts I want you to take as much space as you can in the room you're in. Like the previous John Osborne piece, I want you to create the world of the words in the room. I want you to really see the mother, really see the rhinoceros. I want you to see herds of them across the plains of your room. I want you to be in the brothel and feel the matelot's arm. I want you to move the mother into a corner of the room when she's in the cistern. I want to see the old grey charging horse. See them, feel them, imagine them as if they're are all in the room with you now!
>   OK, go!

This is very tricky to do unless you've learnt the words. I'm sure all the characters were there, some of the time, but maybe occasionally you started to pretend. But if you really believe they're there, a person listening and watching will too.

> If you're up to it, have another go.

This time I'd like you to stay reasonably still, but I'd like you to look to all the places in the room where each character exists as you come to them: the rhinos, the mother, the brothel, the matelot, the old horse and also Jimmy's best friend and his wife!

Your room must have been really buzzing! What I've been asking you to do is to be in each moment as if it's the present. When we tell stories, each moment is relived as if it were happening now. Whenever you talk to someone, in any speech, on any subject, you'll move through past, present, and future in less than a moment.

This time I want you to take the speech to the extreme! I want you to feel as though you're very, very angry! There is a major row going on in your room! Start to move around it, remembering what it feels like to be really angry. Your breathing rate increases. You feel your whole body about to explode. Bring into the room a person who makes your blood boil – bring them in now!

Use the words like a power hammer: very clear, very loud, very slow, but with more energy than you've ever used before. Don't tighten your throat – pump air into the words instead. Use all the skills you've learnt from your vocal exercises to express each word with all the power that it contains. Use the previous exercise to place each image around the room. Allow the words to affect how you feel after you say each thought. Allow your child to hear and react and join in with what you're feeling. Let yourself feel how your child feels.

Hold your ground when you start to speak, stay loose, be really centred, win the row and fly together with your child into the speech.

OK, wow! How was that? You should be feeling emotional, elated and exhausted, all at the same time! Did you find the words helped you to release even more energy? Did you tell the person in the room what you really felt – or did you feel nervous about being so powerful?

It'll take you a few minutes to let the energy and the feelings subside. Allow them to continue to be released. If you really committed to what you were saying, you'll have released a powerful amount of emotional energy. You'll be feeling you've unlocked energy that's been held inside you for years.

You may be wondering, in terms of giving a speech, why I believe you need to do what you've just done? It's because speeches are about energy. What you did, by using anger, was to explore your ability to express emotional energy.

TAKING YOUR SPACE

When I work with people at home I'll ask them to do all of these texts just as you've done them, with all the different emotional triggers. Then I'll open my front door and, as they start to speak, I'll slowly move to the other side of the street. This can be quite embarrassing! The reason I move away is to make the person maintain their connection with me, the listener, over a large distance, not by shouting, but by using more air when they say the words. If they don't have enough air and start to shout, I come back in and we start the speech all over again!

Even though I'm so far away, the basic elements of the perfect conversation still remain. The speaker says the thought, I repeat it under my breath, we share the thought, I indicate I've got it and they move on to the next thought. When they've completed a set of thoughts, we share those too and then we move on. The only difference is that the sound takes a little longer to reach me.

The speakers do, of course, find they're saying the words more slowly with more energy than they would if I were two feet away, but they're still just talking to me. They know they're being heard and we're sharing a 'perfect conversation' – and nothing else matters in the world!

If you can recreate what I do with them, by either flinging open your front door or really starting to imagine speaking in a large space, you'll have the measure of what you'll need to do if you're speaking to a large group of people without a microphone. In fact even if there is one, you'll need to allow the same amount of time for the sound to reach them!

Any of the texts can be used with any of the emotional triggers we've worked with. Don't limit yourself to what I've suggested. Explore them for yourself and create your own. Use your imagination.

I hope one of these texts has really reached you. If it did, and you have the time, it would be brilliant if you learnt it. You'll find you nearly have already! Why? Because it really means something to you, it's touched your child.

Knowing a text will be invaluable in any preparation you do when you next have to speak. Later, when I suggest you go and check out a venue where you may be speaking, possibly before you've prepared what you're going to say, you can use your text to get the measure of the place, to feel your sound in that space.

If you can find a friend you feel happy to try some of these texts out with, fantastic. If not, look at the recordings you've made to see how quickly you've developed. You'll be amazed. If you haven't recorded yourself, just trust your inner ear to tell you how well you've done and how much you've moved towards speaking from the heart instead of the head.

SWEARING AND SCREAMING AND PILLOWS
It is not always easy to find the right words to release locked up emotional energy. Nor is it always easy to find a safe space. Now I'm going to offer up to you two unbelievably powerful methods of releasing some, if not all, of this pent up energy.

In most societies swearing is considered an abuse of the language. Very often, we are told it's the mark of a person who is showing their ignorance and poor education, because they can't find a better way to express themselves. However, virtually everyone uses swear words at some time or other to express feelings and emotions they're finding it impossible to hold in. There are those whose every other word is a swear word. Yet rarely does anyone dare to use them as fully as they could. When they say them, they rarely articulate them in every detail. They'll mumble them out or just make the general sound, diminishing the word's power. They're actually afraid a parent or teacher is going to appear from the past and tell them off! That's why this is so liberating: you'll break the power of the past; you'll break through your own taboos.

These are extremely powerful words, handed on through time to be used sparingly to release pent up emotions! The most effective way of doing this is to articulate them in all their detail and power the sounds with your newfound vocal ability.

I want you to make a list of 10 swear words. The worst you can think of!

When you've made your list, I want you to say them one at a time. Make sure your voice is warm and well limbered up. I want you to say each and every syllable, hitting every consonant for all it's worth.

Say each word three times, to be sure you've wrung out all the detail and power you can from it. Allow a silence and breathe each time you say a word. Allow whatever feelings come up and out to be released. Celebrate your ability to let go of powerful emotions through a word!

You may not, of course, feel there is anywhere 'safe' you can say these words. This is where you can use an item you'll find in your bedroom!

A big soft pillow is great at absorbing sound. You can use it to swear into safely! You'll hear the words in all their detail, but the neighbours won't. You can also use it to scream into!

> Screaming is another wonderful way to release locked up energy. Again, make sure your voice is warm and open before you do it, though, otherwise you'll damage the back of your throat.
> Without tightening up and shouting, scream as loud as you can into a pillow. Feel your whole body vibrate as you release enormous amounts of energy. Feel the incredible power of your voice. Experience your personal vocal **power**.

If you've now completed these practical sections and have been brave enough to risk more than you previously imagined you could, you will without doubt have the physical and emotional ability to talk to any number of people and recreate the perfect conversation each and every time you speak.

I hope you and your child have realized that expressing held in energy is safer than you think. By talking through texts, perhaps you've been able to express some of your child's rage and joy and sadness through your adult voice. You've found you can both free yourself from fear and say what you really feel.

IF

Finally in this section I'm going to give you a poem by Rudyard Kipling called 'If'. It has many of the elements of a speech and is also a lovely poem.

> So now, for the sheer pleasure of it, say the poem as if it were a speech, allowing your child to join in, allowing the words to come from your heart.

IF you can keep your head when all about you
are losing theirs and blaming it on you;
If you can trust yourself when all men doubt you,
But make allowance for their doubting too;
If you can wait and not be tired by waiting,
Or being lied about, not deal in lies,
Or being hated not give way to hating,
And yet don't look too good, nor talk too wise:

IF you can dream – and not make dreams your master;
If you can think of Triumph and Disaster
And treat those two imposters just the same;
If you can bear to hear the truth you've spoken
Twisted by knaves to make a trap for fools,
Or watch the thing you gave your life to, broken,
And stoop and build 'em up with worn out tools:

IF you can make one heap of all your winnings
And risk it on one turn of pitch-and-toss,
And lose, and start again at your beginnings
And never breathe a word about your loss;
If you can force your heart and nerve and sinew
To serve your turn long after they are gone,
And so hold on when there is nothing in you
Except the Will which says to them: 'Hold on!'

IF you can talk with crowds and keep your virtue,
Or walk with kings – nor lose the common touch,
If neither foes or loving friends can hurt you,
If all men count with you, but none too much;
If you can fill the unforgiving minute
With sixty seconds' worth of distance run,
Yours is the earth and everything that's in it,
And – which is more – you'll be a Man, my son.

CHAPTER EIGHT

GETTING UP THERE

Everything you've read and all that you've done so far has been a preparation to recreate the perfect conversation when you give a major speech. 'But,' you may say, 'I'm never going to give a major speech. All I want to be able to do is say what I really mean when I talk to someone!' That's fine. Maybe you need to see your boss about a problem in the office. Maybe you're going for a job interview. Maybe you need to have an important meeting with all of your departmental heads present. Maybe you need to convince your bank manager to give you a loan. Perhaps you want to explain to your lover what you really feel and why, in a way that allows them to stay connected with your words and how you truly feel. A good meeting, a good radio or TV interview, a good discussion, all require exactly the same elements as a major speech.

Of course you could send a letter, write a memo or distribute a report. But it's just not the same, is it? When people meet and really talk to each other, they exchange more than just words – they exchange a part of themselves, their energy, they help to bring each other back into harmony.

That's why we don't go to hear people speak just for the facts we will learn. We can get those out of books. We go to hear and feel their emotional energy – to feel what it's like to be them, to be energized by them and transformed. Well, that's what we hope will happen every time we listen to someone speak.

My wife has quite literally just walked in the door, feeling angry and irritated, having spent the past two and half hours in a meeting which she had to attend at the last minute that was a total waste of her time. What she felt was lacking most, as she sat with the five other people, was emotional energy. The meeting was being run by someone who saw it as an opportunity to think out loud, with no emotional commitment to anything he was saying. He hadn't prepared himself whatsoever. Because he was so dull and lifeless, so was the meeting. Even though my wife tried to inject some energy into the proceedings, she was sucked into the bottomless reservoir of his apathy based on fear.

It sounded very similar to a conference I'd recently been to. The audience had travelled from all over the country to hear this person speak. What we got in return for all the effort and energy we put into being there was a very dull report, which we could have read at our leisure. To be stuck in a room or a conference hall, listening to someone drone on with no means of escape, is a nightmare all of us have had to experience!

Whether you call a meeting, or go for an interview for a new job or agree to stand up in front of a group of people and talk, energy has to be flowing. You need the energy to move your audience. Otherwise, why put yourself through it all? But now let's just remind ourselves of the energy many people actually experience when they get up to talk in front of 3,000 people: **drop-dead gut-wrenching fear.**

FEAR

Fear, as we've already explored, is energy released by adrenalin into your body to deal with a situation which your child has decided from its earliest experiences is frightening, or which is new and out of your child's knowledge and understanding. Both put you into a state of 'fight or flight', creating an overwhelming feeling of disharmony! This energy needs to be released out of your body to bring you back into equilibrium. However, if you neither fight nor flee, but freeze, your energy will remain trapped, your body will shake and you'll start to sweat as your molecules vibrate faster and faster with no release! Know the feeling? Let's call this 'freeze mode'! This is the state most people go into when they're about to speak to 1,000 people plus TV cameras! This is the state your child will get stuck in if they're still torn between staying and saying what's really hurting them or running away.

Some would-be speakers literally do run away, either on the day or before the event. They run away from what frightens them the most – their fear of fear. I remember when I was 10, turning down the part of Joseph in the school nativity play, because I didn't believe I could learn the lines. I ended up playing a star and froze on my first word!

If you actually want to deliver the speech, you're really only left with one way of releasing the energy: fight!

'Fight' means action. You could take it to mean getting violent. That would be a very primitive and basic response to the surge of adrenalin. But it's only one expression of strong emotional energy. Take the word 'passion'. It's defined as: 'a strong emotion; an outburst of anger; sexual love; enthusiasm for something or for doing something'. So, could this 'strong emotion' which your child might interpret as fear, just as easily be experienced and expressed as one the many variations of passion?

Let's imagine you're on your first date with a gorgeous person you've been dying to go out with for ages. How would you be feeling? Would your heart be beating faster? Would the palms of your hands be wringing wet? Would energy be pouring off you? Would adrenalin be pumping through you? Would you feel excited?

You could tell me you'd feel nervous, frightened, terrified. But you'd also be elated, ecstatic and thrilled to be alive!

The energy is exactly the same whether you believe you're terrified or excited. The only difference is what your child thinks it is!

Let's imagine you're passionate about your garden. You put a lot of energy and enthusiasm into making it beautiful. When you look at what you've achieved, you feel really happy. Now if someone messed it all up you'd feel very angry. If the authorities said they were going to compulsorily purchase your garden and build a bypass, you may well express your emotions in the form of anger at what they were planning to do. You'd be a passionate member of the action committee trying to stop them!

There is absolutely no difference between energy experienced as fear and energy experienced as passion. It's what you do with it that matters! So, this surge of energy which your child might so easily interpret as fear could just as easily be experienced and expressed as passion.

If, during the course of our work together, you've managed to unlock some of your child's fears, you'll now be ready to convince each other that all it is is pure energy! And the form in which it will be most usefully employed is passion, because **if you feel no passion, in whatever form, for what you're asking people to listen to, there really is no point in talking. And very little point in anyone listening!**

Fear and passion are both expressions of the same thing – emotional energy that needs to be released to bring you back into harmony. By understanding and accepting this, you will very quickly be able to connect to and transform your energy, instead of being afraid of it!

THE MAGIC MOMENT

Let's say you're giving a speech or talking to a group of people, but still feeling frightened, not passionate. Yet your heart rate is exactly the same as when you felt passionate. How do you convince your child that what you're really feeling is passion?

Now of course it will all depend on what kind of speech you prepared! If there's no emotional energy in your words, you're going to have a big problem! However, if when you were working on the speech you felt some form of passion for what you really wanted to say and if you rehearsed with all the passion you felt for the words, every time you said them, then on the day of the speech, all you need do is allow yourself to listen to and feel the passion you've already put into the words!

Just as you did with the texts, you will trigger the emotional memory of those words every time you say them. If you power those words, using the energy that will surely be flowing when you get up to speak, you will connect to your passion and fly! Your energy will energize your speech instead of 'locking you up'. This magic moment is going to happen, because of all the work you've done and all the preparation you're going to do. Just remember to listen to what you are saying: listen!

If you're listening to the words you prepared – at the very same moment as the audience – all of you will be taken together to the emotions you felt when you first started to think about what you really wanted to say.

But this emotional energy will only be available if you're prepared to risk letting us see and hear your child. If you are determined to keep that part of you hidden, nothing, I repeat nothing, will ever happen when you get up to speak. If you use your energy, however, you'll have the makings of a brilliant speaker – no matter what the subject. I have to say, I heard someone speaking on slime mould once and he was wonderful. He lost none of his authority by sharing with us his childlike enthusiasm for his subject. It was there in everything he said. I was mesmerized. I now know an awful lot more about slime mould than I'd ever have thought possible!

BE PREPARED

The usual excuse for lack of preparation is there's no time. But what's the point in wasting other people's time and energy by not being properly prepared? If you haven't the time, don't bother to do it!

Of course the real reason most people don't prepare properly is because they're afraid. But you and I are going to transform that fear into passion, into an energy you can use every time you talk!

Giving a speech without thoroughly preparing what you want to say and why you want to say it is crazy in the extreme. Nobody can cover for you, nobody can take the attention away from your lack of preparation – you're on your own! Yet many people try to convince themselves it will all 'just happen', magically the words will flow. If you're totally at ease in front of an audience, they will! But if your child suddenly finds you're not prepared for something that terrifies them to death you can be sure they'll take control away from you, just as you start to speak!

MAKING A SPEECH

I'm going to take you through a highly structured preparation for a major written speech. Whether you finally give it using notes or speak off the cuff, by preparing properly and rehearsing thoroughly, you'll transform your fear into a powerhouse of usable energy. It won't be frightening! It'll become one of the most exciting experiences you've ever had in your life – bar none!

Maybe you'll never give a major speech in your life – no matter. Everything you're going to do here can be used in every other speaking situation you're ever likely to find yourself in. The elements are exactly the same, only the scale will be different.

The strange thing is, you'll probably find, in the not too distant future, that someone will ask you to give a major speech or a talk or TV interview! If any of the work we've done together has had an effect, people will start to think of you first when they're looking for someone to talk. There'll be something about you that makes them know you can do it and instead of saying, 'No I can't,' you'll find yourself saying, 'I'd love to!'

PREPARING THE SPEECH

Right, you've been asked to give a major speech on a subject you know and care about. The first thing you'll need is information. Yet, so often, out of fear, people avoid asking the questions they most need answered. It's as if they're trying to pretend it's not going to happen!

But if you don't have the answers to your child's questions, how are you going to calm their fears?

There will be times here when I'll ask you to repeat something you've already done. Please don't skip over it! Not yet! Your rational mind will probably be saying, 'Yes, yes I understand.' But your child won't be so certain and on the day they'll panic! The repeats are their reassurance, so please do them, for their sake.

Remember, you may not be able to do everything I suggest, but the more you can, the less likelihood there'll be of you finding yourself terrified in front of an audience, praying that you were somewhere else and wishing you had properly prepared!

Asking and Listening

Michelangelo, the great artist and sculptor, said that all he had to do was to cut away the rock to find the sculpture hidden inside. He only had to trust that he would find the sculpture which was already lying within the stone, waiting to be brought out into the light of day. The speech you're going to give is already inside you, waiting to be heard. All we're going to do is to bring it into existence. All you'll need to do is to listen until you can hear.

Listening, as we've discovered, is an art in itself. The Chinese character for the verb 'to listen' is made up of five small drawings: 1) the ear; 2) you; 3) the eyes; 4) undivided attention; and 5) the heart. Remember, lousy listeners make lousy speakers!

The Search

First, we need to find the piece of rock you're going to be working with. You'll probably be told which quarry to start looking in by the people who've asked you to speak. They'll give you your 'subject'. But you'll need much more information to find the precise rock you're going to be working with!

To help you locate the speech even more, you'll need to know why they've asked you. What it is they feel you could bring to the speech, that someone else can't? The very fact that they're asking you to do it will tell you that they can already hear elements of what you're going to say, even if you can't!

Also, just as when you're due to meet someone new, it helps if you know who you're going to be talking to. Who are they? You need to know something about them to help you connect, to help you find your common ground, to reassure the children! Knowing where and when and how you're speaking is all part of the information you need for your child to really know and understand what's happening.

These are the main questions you need to know the answers to:

- What's the subject I'm speaking on?
- Why do they want me to speak?
- What's the purpose of the event?
- What's due to happen on the day?
- How's it going to be staged?
- What time of day am I speaking?
- How long will I be expected to speak?
- Who's on before me and what's their subject?
- Who's on after me and what's their subject?
- How many people will I be speaking to?
- Who's going to be in the audience?
- What kind of people are they?
- How knowledgeable are they on the subject?
- What matters to them most about the subject?

Going There

There are also other invaluable ways of preparing yourself for your speech. By going to the venue ahead of time and getting to know the space even before you do anything else, you'll be giving yourself and your child as much information as possible about the event, so that on the day there will be as few shocks as possible. Also, you'll be able to place the speech in time and space.

When actors arrive at their first rehearsal for a stage play, they're shown a model of the set they'll be acting in and if the theatre is available they'll be shown the actual space. They'll have a feel for the 'event' even before they've started to rehearse. It's much better to know what the space is like beforehand, rather than find yourself explaining later, 'I didn't know I'd have to talk over a loud air conditioning system or speak in a room next to the kitchens preparing for lunch! I didn't know I'd have to compete with low flying aircraft!' Recently, I found myself in a venue where the only thing between me and a swimming pool with people shouting and screaming was a thin piece of glass!

The place won't be exactly the same on the day, but if you check it out beforehand, you'll have valuable information about 'locating' the speech you're going to give. You'll have located it in time and space.

Here are the main things to try and do well ahead if you can:

- Go to the space where you'll be speaking.
- Rehearse the journey, ideally at the same time of day.
- Check out where you're going to park.
- Check out where the loos are.
- Check out how you'll get to the platform.
- Imagine the space full of people.
- Try and stand on the exact spot you're going to talk from.
- Say one of the texts we've already worked with.
- Try it using different voices and volume and emotions.
- Throw your voice around the space, feel it come back.
- Imagine the audience being there; breathe into the feeling.
- Talk to your child and let them have a go at speaking.
- If they get nervous, reassure them you'll be with them every step of the way.
- Help them get excited!
- Move around the space. Get to know it. Get comfortable with it.
- Check the acoustics. Is there a noisy air conditioning system?
- Find the particular seat where the 13-year-old girl is going to be, somewhere near the back on the left-hand side of your view.
- Sit in her seat and imagine yourself up on the platform.

- If you can't go to the venue yourself, talk to someone who's been there before.
- *Know* the space.

You've located the speech in time and space. But now you need to select the actual 'rock' you're going to work with! Try and give yourself a few days to get this information together.

- Write down everything about the subject that you believe you might want to talk about.
- Write down everything you believe will matter to your particular audience.
- Gather all the background information you think is truly important to what you believe you want to say.

You now have in place your information, your piece of rock, from which will emerge your speech. Already your mind will be searching for the speech you're going to make. But now try to let it go for a couple of days. Trust that the speech is there waiting to be heard.

GOING WITHIN

A day or two later, come back to your rock as you begin to look inside. You've arrived at the magic stage – allowing the speech to begin to form, allowing the sculpture to emerge! Give yourself the time and space to allow it to happen without interruption.

- Find a quiet time and read through all your notes.
- Think about your audience.
- Sit in your straight-backed chair or lie on the floor with a book under your head and do your 'Letting Go' exercise.

- Go to your safe place and get in touch again with your feelings of well-being.
- Say hello to your child and be in your magic place together.
- From your special place, your safe space, imagine where you and your child will be when you get up to talk.

Picture the scene as vividly as you can by going through all the things your child may need to be reminded of and reassured about.

Gently remind your child:
- Where you'll both be speaking.
- What day you'll both be speaking.
- What time you'll both be speaking.
- Who's going to be there.
- Listen to your child's fears.
- Reassure them you'll look after them.
- Imagine yourselves in the hall about to speak.
- See yourselves actually speaking to the audience.
- See and feel the audience respond.
- Start to feel what really matters, not in words but in emotions, as you hear your tone of voice.
- Start to connect to what really matters to you and your child, what really needs to be said. Whatever emotions you feel, let yourselves feel them.

Ask your child:
- What do we really want to tell them?
- What makes us angry about the situation?
- What are we passionate to change?
- Why do we so want to tell them?
- Why does it matter so much that we tell these people?
- What difference could it make to their lives if they acted on what we say?
- Why does that matter?

- What excites us about what we might achieve?
- What effect on the audience would make us feel fantastic?

What will come first are the emotions surrounding the speech. Allow yourselves to experience these feelings. Remember how much it matters to you and your child that you give this speech. Allow yourselves to believe you can and will change things for the better, using emotions through words to express what you both feel.

When you are truly connected to the passion and purpose of the speech, I want you to write down the answers to these questions – from your guts – about the content of the speech. They may be angry, wicked, naughty, enthusiastic or compassionate feelings. Don't be polite, don't censor yourselves. Say them out loud with all the emotion you're feeling and write them down.

THE KEY QUESTIONS

- What's it really all about?
- What's really happening at the moment?
- What's really not working at the moment?
- What changes must we make?
- What real difference would this make to everyone's lives?
- What will happen if we don't change?
- What's our vision of the ideal future?
- What sums up everything we want to say?
- What's the first step we must take to achieve this better future?

What you've just written down is the emotional structure of the story you're going to tell. Remember, stories are the truth put in a form that everyone can emotionally connect to. People do not connect to facts, but to emotions. Now leave what you've written down for a day and a night.

Now you're going to cut away the bulk of the rock surrounding your sculpture, allowing those emotions you've brought to the surface to roam free in you.

ADDING THE DETAIL

- Find a quiet time and read through all your notes.
- Think about your audience.
- Sit in your straight-backed chair or lie on the floor with a book under your head and do your 'Letting Go' exercise.
- Go to your safe place and get in touch again with your feelings of well-being.
- Say hello to your child and be in your magic place together.
- From your special place, your safe space, imagine where you and your child will be, when you get up to talk.

- Gently remind your child:
  - Where you'll both be speaking.
  - What day you'll both be speaking.
  - What time you'll both be speaking.
  - Who's going to be there.
  - Listen to your child's fears.
  - Reassure them you'll look after them.

- Imagine yourselves actually giving the speech or the talk.
- See and hear yourselves actually speaking to the audience.
- See and feel the audience respond.
- Connect to what really matters to you, your child and the audience.
- Feel and hear what really matters in words and emotions.
- Whatever emotions you feel, let yourselves feel them.

- Go to your desk and read through your answers to the key questions.
    - Write down the facts which are relevant to your answers, but with the same level of emotion. Don't censor yourselves. Enjoy getting it out of your system!
    - Add any stories which bring the emotions you're feeling even more alive.
    - Give examples which will matter to you, your child and your audience.
    - Forget about it all for at least a day and a night.

It will be tempting to try and start to write out the speech now, but it really does pay to leave it and think about and do other things. When you come back to it, something will have happened. Even though you've been elsewhere, the complete speech will be ready to emerge when you come back to it.

WRITING IT OUT

- A day or two later, find a quiet time and read through your latest notes.
- Think about your audience.
- Sit in your straight-backed chair or lie on the floor with a book under your head and do your 'Letting Go' exercise.
- Go to your safe place and get in touch again with your feelings of well-being.
- Say hello to your child and be in your magic place together.
- From your special place, your safe space, imagine where you and your child will be, when you get up to talk.

- Remind your child:
  - Where you'll both be speaking.
  - What day you'll both be speaking.
  - What time you'll both be speaking.
  - Who's going to be there.
  - Listen to your child's fears.
  - Reassure them you'll look after them.
  - Imagine yourselves again actually giving the speech or the talk.

- It's as if you are both hearing and seeing the future.
- Feel yourselves actually speaking to the audience.
- See and feel them respond.
- Enjoy the feeling of being truly heard.
- Start to feel your opening feelings.
- Start to hear the words, as you felt them when you wrote them down. Breathe into and feel the emotions.
- Be there in your mind's eye.
- See the 13-year-old girl sitting towards the back on the left.
- Be in her seat and watch yourselves telling your story with honesty, compassion, humour, anger, enthusiasm – but most of all with passion.
- Know that she is hearing and feeling what you and your child really want to say.

Go Back to your Speech

Now you must choose how direct you're going to be with your audience. Remember, if you truly believe in what you're saying, however much some people won't like it, most of those present will at least respect your integrity for speaking from the heart. Your words and emotions will be heard by the child inside every single person you'll be talking to. Their adult side may try and reject what you say, but their frightened child will have heard. You will have made a real difference to their lives.

This is a spoken text, not a written report. It's written down the way you speak. Remember, we don't speak in sentences. We speak in images and thoughts. See each thought, feel each thought as you write it down. You want every person in the room to understand what you really mean, so using jargon which only ten per cent of the audience understands is a meaningless waste. So too is using complicated language and words that you don't normally use! The words shouldn't get in the way of the emotions. They're there to carry them!

Facts must not get in the way either! Too many facts will overwhelm the speech. Facts only mean something to the audience if they're emotionally connected. If you need to get lots of facts across, hand out a sheet of paper. If you've inspired them to care about what you're saying, they'll read them; if you haven't, they'll go in the bin!

- Gently go to your desk and write out the full text of what you're going to say.
- Say it out loud as you write it down.
- Leave it for a day and a night.

Editing

This part of the work can all too easily be when you censor everything you really wanted to say and replace it with what you think you ought to say! It's up to you, but the closer what you say is to what you really feel, the more you'll be able to change things for the better, the more you will move yourself and your audience to their natural state of harmony.

- A day or two later, find a quiet time and read through what you've written.

- Sit in your straight-backed chair or lie on the floor with a book under your head and do your relaxation.
- Go to your safe place and get in touch again with your feeling of well-being.
- Say hello to your child and just be in your magic place together.
- From your special place, your safe space, imagine where you and your child will be, when you get up to talk.

- Gently remind your child:
  - Where you'll both be speaking.
  - What day you'll both be speaking.
  - What time you'll both be speaking.
  - Who's going to be there.
  - Listen to your child's fears.
  - Reassure them you'll look after them.
  - Imagine yourselves again actually giving the speech or the talk.

- It's as if you are both hearing and seeing the future.
- Feel yourselves actually speaking to the audience.
- See and feel them respond.
- Enjoy the feeling of being truly heard.
- Start to feel your opening feelings.
- Start to hear the words as you felt them when you wrote them down. Breathe into and feel the emotions.
- Be there in your mind's eye.
- See the 13-year-old girl sitting towards the back on the left.
- Be in her seat and watch yourselves telling your story with honesty, compassion, humour, anger, enthusiasm – but most of all with passion.
- Know that she's hearing and feeling what you and your child really want to say.

STAND AND DELIVER

- Gently stand up and say what you've written out loud.
  See the young girl watching and listening and say it to her.
- Any part that doesn't feel right will become clear to you,
  the girl and your child.
- Go to your desk and refine and edit what you've written.

Length

Most speeches are too long! Boringly, impossibly long! Seven minutes is ideal for a formal speech. Twenty is the maximum for an informal speech. If your speech is any longer, you'd better have a very good reason for it and you'd better be incredibly fit! Virtually no one has the stamina to give an inspired speech any longer than I've suggested, unless they are very, very experienced and very, very fit. So I suggest you start with shorter speeches! As you grow in confidence and stamina, you can allow the speeches to grow in length, but only a little!

Laying It Out

As far as the practical layout of your words is concerned, firstly, make sure you can read them clearly. Remember, you will have the pages on a lectern and they'll be further away from you than usual. I suggest a font size of at least 14.

Do not type your speech out in capital letters. They're impossible to read! Use a line spacing of 1.5 or 2. Lay the speech out in thoughts, just as we did in the texts. Add in the commas just as I did. If you and your child get over-'excited', you'll have the hooks in place to get you back onto the text. Underline key verbs and nouns you want to be certain of highlighting. Make sure, where possible, you turn pages at the end of a major point, not in the middle of one, even if it means having more pages. That way, the pause as you turn won't stop the flow of what you're saying and feeling.

Here seems a good point to discuss alternatives to using a written text when you deliver your speech. However, please remember that the preparation and rehearsal need to be just as detailed.

Using Notes

Some people would say giving a speech with notes is harder than giving a written speech. It does take a great deal of confidence to stand up without the support of a script, but it is easier to make a direct connection to your audience. It feels more immediately natural, even if it's easier to run out of things to say! That's why it's crucial to follow exactly the same stages you did when preparing the written speech. In some respects you need to know what you intend to say even more thoroughly!

The key questions will still remain your emotional story structure:

- What's it really all about?
- What's really happening at the moment?
- Why isn't it working at the moment?
- What changes must we make?
- What real difference would this make to everyone's lives?
- What will happen if we don't change?
- What's our vision of the ideal future?
- What sums up everything we want to say?
- What's the first step we must take to achieve this better future?

Also put in place the triggers for:

- The facts which are relevant to your answers.
- The stories which bring the emotions you're feeling even more alive.
- The examples which matter to you and your audience.

- Learn your opening words and fire them with the energy you'll be feeling on the day.

- Remember to listen to what you're actually saying rather than worrying about what you're going to say next!

This emotional story structure and the triggers are just as valid for a meeting, a TV interview or a discussion with your partner about your future. The key questions are exactly the same. You may not answer them in exactly the same order, but you'll probably find that you do, especially if the exchange is to be both fulfilling and meaningful.

If you wish to reduce what you're going to say down to cue cards, which are about the size of postcards, make sure you can read them clearly. You don't want to be holding them in front of your face! Tie them together in case you drop them and have a spare set in your pocket.

Reduce the words down to the minimum you need to remind you of each stage of what you want to say. By using the list above, you'll have a direct connection to your original gut feelings. If you're listening well to your audience, they will let you know when you can expand any given element or contract those which feel on the day of less value. Your speech should have the feel of an 'open rehearsal' where anything can happen within the structure you've created.

OFF THE CUFF

If you are someone who cannot even bear to have cue cards, the rehearsal process is ever more valuable in focusing your mind on what you want to say. I do, however, suggest you learn the key questions. Here's a sentence which may help you remember:

It's about, the moment, not working, but changes,
make a difference, but if we don't, the vision, sums up,
the first step!

REHEARSE, REHEARSE, REHEARSE

Rehearsals are the incredibly exciting stage where all the exercises you've done in the past will really pay off. The more times you say your speech out loud the better. The more often you allow yourself to connect with the passions you felt when you wrote it, the better. Allow yourself to enjoy doing it!

Also, the speech needs to remain fresh and alive. If you're listening and connecting emotionally to the words you're saying over and over, new thoughts will occur to you, new ways of saying what you want to say. Make any changes which connect you even more closely to what you really feel. However, as you grow in confidence, you'll be tempted to elaborate too much. Try not to! See whether fewer words and more energy will improve what you're saying. Edit ruthlessly. If you're really connected to what you're saying, there'll be no need for more explanation. Many people say too much to avoid saying what they really feel!

If you can sometimes rehearse in the space where you're going to be giving the speech, great. By connecting the space to your speech in rehearsals, when you arrive on the day, the space will also help to trigger what you feel.

If you can't use the space itself for rehearsals, use the largest space you can. If you can't find a large space, work at home and warn the family and neighbours! If you've allowed yourself to be excited about what you're saying, they'll enjoy it too! If you go weird on them and get all embarrassed, so will they. It's not easy finding a space to work, but it has to become part of your new bravery.

If you're able to learn your opening and closing words, it will be even easier to power them with the energy you'll be feeling on the day!

Whenever possible, do your 'Letting Go' relaxation and 'Today's the Day' imagination before you start. Also make certain you've done your vocal warm up exercises.

REHEARSALS

- Read out loud your favourite text of those we've worked on.
- Articulate every word in all its detail.
- Add an 'ah' to each word to be certain you are completing it

and to feel your vocal power.

- Have your favourite text and the speech you're going to give in your hand at the same time.
- Imagine the young child is in the room and you're going to move around, 'living' every word you say.
- Start by saying your favourite text.
- If you talk about someone, go to where they are.
- Bring the speech alive.
- Dramatize every moment for the child to see and hear your speech in vivid colour and stereo sound!
- Use the space!
- Around halfway through, move over to your speech, sustaining the same vocal and emotional energy.

- Have your favourite text and the speech you're going to give in your hand at the same time.
- Start by saying your favourite text. Moving over to the speech halfway through.
- Repeat what you've just done, but this time pick a totally over the top accent. (Mine is a mad East European professor!) Articulate every word, allowing your voice and tone and rhythm to change how the words come out. Go overboard!. Stand reasonably still, but see and hear everything. Make it all as vivid as possible. Enjoy.

- Standing, same procedure. Start with your favourite text and move on to the speech.
- Begin in your normal voice, but this time say it to someone who's not listening. You are going to damn well make them listen! Grow in power without your voice going higher or

tighter. Power from your tummy.

- Sit down and quietly start your favourite text as if you are saying it to your best friend. Halfway through, move over to your speech.
- Make sure your friend understands each thought before you move on, breathe between each thought. There is no hurry.
- Allow the elements of the previous versions to affect the way you are saying it now. Each version has something to add. Each version helps to connect you with your passionate energy.

- Stand again and begin your speech from the beginning, as if you were on the spot where you are going to deliver it on the day.
- Breathe into the feeling.
- Imagine looking into some of the audience's eyes.
- See and feel the child in them.
- Feel their energy.
- Find the 13-year-old girl sitting at the back on the left and begin.
- Power the first few words with clarity and passion.
- Allow the speech to start to say itself.
- Breathe between each thought and image.
- Listen to every word you say.
- Allow yourself to re-create the perfect conversation – and fly.

What I've given you is some basic rehearsal structures which you can play around with. If you want to imagine any of the ways you delivered texts earlier in our work together, use them. It's your speech!

USING A TELEPROMPTER
This is for those of you who may be persuaded to put your written speech on this remarkably simple and clever piece of technology

which if you can master it, is wonderful to use, but if you don't will destroy your speeches! A teleprompter passes the words in front of your eyes through a piece of glass. If you focus on the glass you can see the words or, if you look through it, you can either see the lens of a TV camera or the audience, depending on which medium you're using. For it to work well for you, it needs a lot more preparation than most people are prepared to give. So if you are going to use one, make sure you get lots of practice first. Don't imagine you'll be able to walk in on the day and just do it!

The trickiest problem is trusting the person who'll be moving the words in front of your eyes! Remember, you're leading, not them! You really must practise with them beforehand, even if it's only once. They need to hear you say the speech at the correct pace.

The other big problem is that the layout of the words is totally different from the layout you'd normally put on a page. Each line will contain only about five words. What usually happens is that you find the line break comes in exactly the wrong place and breaks up your thoughts!

If you have laid out your speech in thoughts as I've suggested and you can get access to the person who's loading your words onto the teleprompter, make sure wherever possible the layout is easy to make sense of.

Here's a piece of text we've already done, laid out based on around five words per line.

Aboard Air Force One,
President Bush, signed,
the Aid Bill, on his way,
to South Carolina.

Arriving, at dawn,
he was to see,
one of the worst hit states.
But even though,

the debris,
was being cleared,
it's the human problems,
authorities, must now face.
In this state alone,
60,000, are homeless,
half a million, displaced,
and almost 300,000,
out of work.

I can assure you this really does work and makes an amazing difference. As you'll remember, you don't read ahead of what you're saying, so you don't need to see the rest of the sentence! If you pause at any of the commas, it will still make perfect sense. If you pause in the middle of a thought, however, we'll be only too aware that you're reading the words.

A small note: make sure you have a written copy of your text in front of you. Technology can all too easily go wrong!

These techniques will only help you if you still remember to talk through the words to the people on the other side of the screen. The 13-year-old girl is still there waiting for you to talk to her!

THE NIGHT BEFORE

The night before, it will be tempting to do a last minute panic and start doubting all the work you've done. DON'T.

DO:

- The 'Letting Go'.
- The 'Today's the Day' imagination of a major speech, putting yourself as vividly as you can into the feeling of the success you and your child are going to be.
- The speech quietly, thought by thought, reconnecting with the emotion that is held within the words you've prepared.
- Make sure you've gone through everything you'll need for the

following day.

- Check with your child to see whether there is anything they're still worrying about.
- Forget about it all and do something that you enjoy doing.
- Sleep well.

TODAY IS THE DAY!

I hope you've been doing 'Today's the Day' imagination from time to time, not just in preparation for this major speech, but as part of your confidence building. Today it's a physical reality! The speech you give will be just as you've imagined.

Give yourself the time to do the 'Letting Go' and then get up and follow what you've been imagining today would be like as closely as you can.

- Go through 'Letting Go'.
- Go through 'Today's the Day' and live it step by step.
- If you're able to give yourself a full dress rehearsal at least an hour beforehand, do so.
- The least you need to do is a highly articulated word run with a 'warm' voice.
- Have a spare copy of what you've prepared in your pocket or somewhere at hand! You never know when you might leave the original in the loo – at home!
- If you're giving the speech at a time when you usually feel hungry, make sure you've had something to eat well ahead, so that all your blood is not in your stomach.
- Don't eat chocolate or biscuits as they clog your throat!
- Don't have alcohol. It doesn't help, but hinders everything.
- Don't have any caffeine or sugar or you'll be on the ceiling!
- Allow yourself to be brilliant!
- Remember you are having a perfect conversation with friends.

When they say it was wonderful, say thank you.

And don't forget to say thank you to your child and the young girl at the back.

You couldn't have done it without them.

AND FINALLY. . .

Remember, this book is only the beginning! Everything we've done together has been to awaken in you your true potential. This book is here to remind you of what you've already achieved and what you will achieve with a little ongoing effort! The rest is up to you! Just as for a great opera singer or a great athlete, it takes a little practice to move towards perfection! Regular and daily practice! Little and often! OK?

Speech is a gift we are given and talking is a gift we can share. The sound we make is all part of the interconnected web of energy that joins us all together, from the call of the whale to the cry of a baby to the beating of your heart. The sounds and words you use affect us all.

I promise you, however good it feels now, if you continue to develop your physical and emotional strength by returning regularly to the imaginations and exercises here it will only get better and better.

If there's someone you know who might benefit from what we've been doing together, please tell them about the book or, even better, buy it for them! Maybe make it a private present from one friend to another. Share the energy! We desperately need more people in this world who talk honestly and openly from the heart!

Now your energy is altering and your life changing! Every person you meet, every relationship you have, is being transformed through hearing and feeling your rediscovered voice. You've already begun to use your new-found vocal power to affect change for good. You've already started to inspire those around you with your re-found confidence and passion. You've already started to move towards your natural state of harmony and begun truly to find your place in this world. You really are making a difference.

It won't have been easy for you. Using your old voice will have felt all too comfortable. You knew it very well. Like a huge old overcoat you've always worn to keep out the cold, the thought of taking it off will have severely depleted your 'comfort zone' – until you realized that with it on, no one knew who you were! All they saw was your shabby old coat. All they could hear was an exhausted voice locked in a time warp. But the sun was warmer than you thought! The words of others were warmer than you imagined.

By connecting to that part of you which has been longing and waiting to be heard, by listening and caring, you'll have given your child back their natural dignity and their right to live a full and happy life. They in return will have given you back your magic! Together you have found the courage to begin again allowing the world to see and hear who you really are. Together, you can say anything. No one can hurt you. You have nothing to fear.

By learning to listen from a different place you've also started to hear the true voices of those you meet on the next stage of your journey through this life. Each voice will be saying the same thing we all ask of each other: 'Just talk to me...' And it all begins with how you say 'hello'. Whether it's the next person you meet in the street, a gathering of hundreds at a conference, an audience of millions on television or a friend who needs your care and attention, all will be touched and moved by what you say. And so will I! Remember the trampoline? Your energy will reach me. Your true and private voice will be heard. Your love will be shared. It will make us all feel well.

May your energy flow.

It would be good, bearing in mind what I say in **And Finally**, to send a copy of the book direct to a friend via HarperCollins mail order.

JUST TALK TO ME...   0 7225 3005 6   £6.99   □

To order direct just tick the titles you want and fill in the form below:

Name: _____

Address: _____

_____

_____ Postcode: _____

Send to: Thorsons Mail Order, Dept 3, HarperCollins*Publishers*, Westerhill Road, Bishopbriggs, Glasgow G64 2QT.

Please enclose a cheque or postal order or your authority to debit your Visa/Access account—

Credit card no: _____

Expiry date: _____

Signature: _____

—to the value of the cover price plus:

UK & BFPO: Add £1.00 for the first book and 25p for each additional book ordered. **Overseas orders including Eire:** Please add £2.95 service charge. Books will be sent by surface mail but quotes for airmail despatches will be given on request.

24 HOUR TELEPHONE ORDERING SERVICE FOR ACCESS/VISA CARD-HOLDERS—TEL: 0141 772 2281.

JUST TALK TO ME...THE AUDIO TAPE

If you would like an audio tape of the 'Letting Go' and the 'imaginations' recorded by Peter Settelen, please fill in the form below:

Name: _____

Address: _____

_____

Postal or Zip Code _____

Send to: CHAKRA Presentations
            38 Magnolia Road
            Strand on the Green
            London W4 3QN
            England

Please enclose a cheque or postal order (or international money order, if outside UK) made payable to CHAKRA Presentations to the value of £9.99 (this includes postage and packing).